Department of Defense
MANUAL

DoD Integrated Materiel Management (IMM) for Consumable Items: Supply Support Requests (SSRs)

Department of Defense

MANUAL

NUMBER 4140.26-M, Volume 6
September 24, 2010

USD(AT&L)

SUBJECT: DoD Integrated Materiel Management (IMM) for Consumable Items: Supply Support Requests (SSRs)

References: See Enclosure 1

1. PURPOSE

a. <u>Manual</u>. This Manual is composed of several volumes, each containing its own purpose. In accordance with the authority in DoD Directive (DoDD) 5134.12 (Reference (a)), the purpose of the overall Manual is to reissue DoD 4140.26-M (Reference (b)), to provide requirements and procedures consistent with DoDD 4140.1 (Reference (c)), for integrated materiel managers and others who work within or with the DoD supply system to determine if an item qualifies for wholesale management; submitting and processing SSRs, and submitting and processing logistic reassignment (LR) transactions.

b. <u>Volume</u>. This Volume establishes uniform guidance for IMM processes and management controls dealing with SSR processes and procedures; recording of user interest, to include applicable civilian agencies on integrated materiel manager-managed National Stock Number (NSN) items; and identifying DoD Components' demands for NSN and part-numbered items.

2. APPLICABILITY. This Volume applies to:

a. OSD, the Military Departments, the Office of the Chairman of the Joint Chiefs of Staff and the Joint Staff, the Combatant Commands, the Office of the Inspector General of the Department of Defense, the Defense Agencies, the DoD Field Activities, and all other organizational entities within the Department of Defense (hereafter referred to collectively as the "DoD Components").

b. Federal agency organizations participating with the DoD Components, e.g., the U.S. Coast Guard (USCG), Federal Aviation Administration (FAA), and General Services Administration (GSA), but only when and to the extent they adopt the terms of this Manual.

3. DEFINITIONS. See Glossary.

4. POLICY. According to Reference (c), it is DoD policy that the materiel management functions shall be implemented with DoD standard data systems.

5. RESPONSIBILITIES. See Enclosure 2.

6. PROCEDURES. See Enclosure 3.

7. RELEASABILITY. UNLIMITED. This Volume is approved for public release and is available on the Internet from the DoD Issuances Website at http://www.dtic.mil/whs/directives.

8. EFFECTIVE DATE. This Volume is effective upon its publication to the DoD Issuances Website.

Alan F. Estevez
Principal Deputy Assistant Secretary of Defense
for Logistics and Materiel Readiness

Enclosures
    1. References
    2. Responsibilities
    3. Procedures
    4. SSR Control Elements and Timeframes Objectives
    5. Use of SIASCN
    Glossary

TABLE OF CONTENTS

TABLES

CONTENTS

ENCLOSURE 1

REFERENCES

(a) DoD Directive 5134.12, "Deputy Under Secretary of Defense for Logistics and Materiel Readiness (DUSD(L&MR))," May 25, 2000

(b) DoD 4140.26-M, "Defense Integrated Materiel Management Manual for Consumable Items," May 16, 1997 (cancelled by Volume 1 of this Manual)

(c) DoD Directive 4140.1, "Supply Chain Materiel Management Policy," April 22, 2004

(d) Executive Order 13423, "Strengthening Federal Environmental, Energy, and Transportation Management," January 26, 2007

(e) Council on Environmental Quality Memorandum, "Implementation Instructions and Requirements for Executive Order 13423," March 28, 2007

(f) DoD 4100.39-M, "Federal Logistics Information System (FLIS) Procedures Manual," dates vary by volume

(g) Military Standard MIL-PRF-49506, "Logistics Management Information," U.S Army Logistics Support Agency Acquisition Support Center, January 18, 2005

(h) Subparts 206.3 and 227.7102-1 of the Defense Federal Acquisition Regulation Supplement, current edition

(i) Section 2320 of title 10, United States Code

(j) Joint Publication 1-02, "Department of Defense Dictionary of Military and Associated Terms," current edition

ENCLOSURE 2

RESPONSIBILITIES

1. <u>ASSISTANT SECRETARY OF DEFENSE FOR LOGISTICS AND MATERIEL READINESS (ASD(L&MR))</u>. The ASD(L&MR), under the authority, direction, and control of the Under Secretary of Defense for Acquisition, Technology, and Logistics (USD(AT&L)), shall oversee SSR procedures to optimize resources and leverage collaboration between support providers and customers to meet established support strategies.

2. <u>SECRETARIES OF THE MILITARY DEPARTMENTS; DIRECTORS OF DEFENSE LOGISTICS AGENCY (DLA) AND NATIONAL SECURITY AGENCY (NSA); AND THE COMMANDANT, UNITED STATES COAST GUARD (USCG) AND ADMINISTRATORS OF OTHER FEDERAL AGENCIES (e.g., FAA AND GSA)</u>. The Secretaries of the Military Departments; the Directors of DLA and NSA; and the Commandant, USCG and Administrators of other Federal agencies (FAA and GSA) when agreed to by these agencies, shall:

    a. Implement the procedures in this Volume.

    b. Select best value and lifecycle materiel support alternatives for meeting customer materiel requirements.

    c. Ensure that cognizant materiel managers actively interface with the program manager and participate as early as feasible for each weapon system acquisition program to ensure effective provisioning support of the warfighter.

    d. Conform with item management criteria in assigning integrated materiel managers.

ENCLOSURE 3

PROCEDURES

1. <u>OPERATIONAL REQUIREMENTS PROCESSES</u>. In terms of the operational requirements processes in this Volume:

a. SSRs shall be transmitted electronically and processing shall adhere to the procedures contained in this Volume. SSR procedures apply to consumable items subject to item management assignment to an integrated materiel manager, including:

(1) Items already managed by an integrated materiel manager.

(2) New items being assigned to an integrated materiel manager for the first time.

(3) Initial and follow-on supply support requirements.

(4) Items previously used only by a foreign country but which U.S. forces subsequently require.

(5) Items that require reinstatement or reactivation.

b. SSR procedures do NOT currently apply to:

(1) Medical materiel.

(2) Clothing and textiles.

(3) Subsistence items.

(4) Fuels.

(5) Ammunition.

(6) Items used by a foreign country but not used by U.S. forces.

(7) Non-consumable items.

(8) Nuclear ordnance items.

c. In accordance with Executive Order 13423 (Reference (d)) and the implementing memorandum (Reference (e)), "green" products or services must be considered as the first choice in all procurements, except those products or services procured for combat or combat-related missions. The IMM, after coordination with the Military Services or Departments, may add new, environmentally preferable "green" items that are an equal alternative to the existing non-environmentally friendly "brown" items currently in the inventory.

2. <u>SSR SUBMISSIONS</u>. The SSR process updates catalog data in the Federal Logistics Information System (FLIS) database, establishes new NSNs in FLIS, and communicates new or changed requirements for consumable items, retail and wholesale, to the integrated materiel manager.

   a. <u>Military Department SSR Submissions</u>

     (1) <u>SSR Formats</u>. These procedures address standardized formats, data elements, coding instructions, engineering data for provisioning (EDFP) requirements, controls, validation, file maintenance, and transmission. Each SSR format communicates events or actions that occur during the SSR process. SSRs are categorized into major types based on these events and actions. The transactions are the primary inputs to and outputs from the SSR process.

       (a) Through the use of document identifier codes (DICs) and SSR action-taken codes (ATCs) (see Tables 1 and 2 of the appendix to this enclosure), a submitter may request that an action be taken or an SSR receiver may communicate an action that has been taken.

       (b) SSR submitters will use standard edit and validation procedures and criteria and the codes and formats contained in the tables of this Volume, and will correct invalid data conditions and resubmit SSRs, as appropriate.

     (2) <u>Item Entry Control (IEC)</u>

       (a) Prior to submitting SSRs, preparers will perform item identification functions to ensure the correct identification of items of supply. Preparers also will review item identifying information, commercial and Government entity (CAGE) code reference number, unit of issue (UI), item name, EDFP, and screen each item against FLIS under the procedures in DoD 4100.39-M (Reference (f)). Match conditions will be reviewed, determinations of "standard," "alternate," "replacement," "substitute," or "cancelled" accomplished, and items identified to the correct NSN and integrated materiel manager.

       (b) When probable or possible matches from the FLIS database are not technically acceptable, the SSR submitter will use the appropriate reference number justification code (RNJC) contained in Reference (f).

     (3) <u>SSR Submission Conditions</u>. SSRs will be submitted to cover:

       (a) Initial requests to record a user for new and existing NSN items.

       (b) Subsequent submission of SSRs as initial or change transactions to cover:

         <u>1</u>. Equipment design changes.

        <u>2</u>. Follow-on provisioning of the same equipment from the same contractor under a different contract.

        <u>3</u>. Re-provisioning of the same equipment from a different contractor under a different contract.

        <u>4</u>. Requirements for the same equipment from a different contractor under the same contract with equipment deliveries spread across 2 or more years.

        <u>5</u>. Requirements for items not originally provisioned that are generated from requisition processing or requests for support from field activities.

        <u>6</u>. Requirements for different equipment that use the same parts.

    (4) <u>Support of Requirements</u>. The SSR submitters or their field units, in support of their requirements submitted on SSRs, will:

        (a) Forward funded requisitions to the integrated materiel manager for retail quantities of items.

        (b) Budget for and procure support quantities as required to support retail if required to support fielded equipment until the support date indicated in the accept advice transaction.

        (c) Submit a design change notice (DCN) to show adjustment in requirements when the initial requirement is found to be erroneous or no longer needed.

   b. <u>SSR Submitting Agency or Activity Responsibilities</u>. The SSR submitting agency or activity will:

    (1) Maintain SSR submission records.

        (a) Retain documentation showing how the forecast quantities were computed for at least 3 years after the support date.

        (b) Review data provided by the integrated materiel manager to determine the cause when actual demand varies from the forecast quantities and initiate action to improve future forecasts, as appropriate.

        (c) Perform systemic data exchanges when adjustments to forecast quantities are required.

    (2) Perform the following actions in submitting requests.

        (a) An SSR requesting support for NSN items is identified by document identifier codes (DICs) CWA or CXA and contains the information required to process the item. This information includes SSR control elements, item management data, and requirements data. NSN requests will be prepared under the instructions contained in Tables 4 through 6 in the appendix to this enclosure. NSN requests fall into one of two categories: a Condition 1 SSR or a Condition 2 SSR. The Condition 1 SSR is a request for support for an NSN managed by an integrated materiel manager.

(b) The Condition 2 SSR is a request for support for an NSN that has no recorded integrated materiel manager in the FLIS database, or recorded Service users. SSRs will be posted to SSR files and controls established to ensure the receipt of advice from the integrated materiel manager. Support advice will be provided by the integrated materiel manager within allowed timeframes (Table 27). If the support advice has not been received, a follow-up will be sent to the integrated materiel manager.

(c) An SSR requesting support for P/N items, referred to as a Condition 3 SSR, is identified by DIC CXB and contains the full range of cataloging and management data required for the integrated materiel manager or designated agent to obtain an NSN. These requests will be prepared in accordance with procedures and format in Tables 7 and 8 of the appendix to this enclosure. Submittal of EDFP is required for all CXB transactions (see Table 40 of Reference (f) for CAGE codes that require no data submission with SSR).

(d) Quantities needed to support participating Service requirements when acting as the Executive Service during joint Service provisioning are included.

(3) Submit EDFP.

(a) <u>Submission Process</u>. EDFP approved at provisioning is required as part of the SSR submission process for:

<u>1</u>. Technical identification of items for maintenance support considerations.

<u>2</u>. Preparation of item identification for the purpose of assigning NSNs.

<u>3</u>. Review for IEC.

<u>4</u>. Standardization.

<u>5</u>. Review for potential interchangeability and substitutability.

<u>6</u>. Item management code (IMC).

(b) <u>Submission Requirements</u>. When available, EDFP will be submitted for all initial SSRs requesting NSN assignment. When EDFP is not available, the item will be identified at least by CAGE and a definitive reference number, item name (DIC CXF), and UI to permit NSN assignment. Assignment of the technical data justification code (TDJC) in the request transaction indicates the reason documentation is not provided for an item.

(c) <u>Order of Precedence</u>. See MIL-PRF-49506 (Reference (g)) for logistics product data guidance. If EDFP is not available, submit SSRs with DIC CXF, item name. When additional reference numbers are available, submit DIC CXG(s).

(4) Process special requirements.

(a) <u>Sole Source Justification</u>. A justification statement will be provided by the SSR submitter as required by subpart 206.3 of the Defense Federal Acquisition Regulation Supplement (DFARS) (Reference (h)), for sole-source procurement of items.

(b) <u>Non-Definitive UI Description</u>. When the UI for a new item is non-definitive, the EDFP will reveal the quantitative measure for the UI. For example, if the unit is a tube, and the tube contains 5 ounces of material, the EDFP will indicate that the tube contains 5 ounces. If the UI is sheet, the dimensions of the sheet will be provided. If a non-definitive UI is received without the required quantitative measure, the SSR will be rejected using ATC 70.

(c) <u>Non-Definitive Reference Numbers</u>. When the reference number submitted for a new item is non-definitive, reference number variation code (RNVC) 1, the EDFP will provide the necessary descriptive information for the integrated materiel manager or designated agent to accomplish stock numbering actions. For example, when the reference number submitted is a non-definitive (RNVC 1) specification item, the engineering data for provisioning shall provide descriptive characteristics of the item, e.g., type, style, color, dimensions, and other data as required by the ordering data section of the specification, but as a minimum it shall provide definitive identification of dimensional, material, mechanical, electrical, and/or other characteristics that depict the physical characteristics, location, and function of the item.

(5) Annotate the contract number under which the EDFP was procured, if appropriate, and the right to use (or restrictions) on drawings and other documentation. Provide the SSR submitter and IMM Activity codes, provisioning control code (PCC), item serial number (ISN), and date of request (DOR) to facilitate filing and matchup of the EDFP with SSR transactions.

(6) Transmit the SSR transaction via DLA Transaction Services and receive acknowledgement of receipt.

(7) Provide a point of contact for each SSR to facilitate problem resolution.

(8) Provide an established acquisition method code (AMC) and acquisition method suffix code (AMSC), at no cost to integrated materiel manager, which allows for immediate procurement of items on SSR. The AMC/AMSC 0/0, while a valid code combination, does not establish the acquisition method and delays the procurement cycle. To optimize the SSR process and minimize procurement delays, the Military Departments will eliminate SSR submissions with an AMC/AMSC 0/0, where possible. If assistance is required in establishing an AMC/AMSC that ensures valid procurement combinations, contact the Engineering Support Office of the Military Department responsible for configuration management of the item.

3. <u>DLA TRANSACTION SERVICES PROCESSING OF SSR SUBMISSIONS</u>. DLA Transaction Services will perform the following actions for SSRs messages submitted by Service users.

    a. Receive and acknowledge receipt of new SSR messages from the Military Departments.

    b. Identify the responsible integrated materiel manager for the submitted SSR.

    c. Forward the SSR to the responsible integrated materiel manager.

    d. Transmit SSR messages from integrated materiel managers to the submitting Service.

4. <u>IMM SSR RECEIPT PROCESSING</u>. The integrated materiel manager or designated agent will:

    a. Receive SSR package and send acknowledgement through DLA TRANSACTION SERVICES.

    b. Provide visibility of process to originator.

    c. When the SSR is received, the integrated materiel manager will perform IEC using available resources including provisioning screenings, internal files, catalogs, EDFP from the SSR submitter, etc. Whenever possible, the result of IEC will be used to accept, offer a substitute, or reroute an item to the correct integrated materiel manager rather than rejecting the item back to the submitter for resubmission. Similarly, inactive and terminal items will be reactivated or reinstated, whenever possible, if a standard, replacement, or substitute item is not available.

    d. Prepare Federal item identification descriptions for new items entering the supply system using the EDFP received from the SSR submitter, its own files, or obtained from contractors. NSNs will be obtained and provided to the SSR submitter.

    e. Determine the range and quantity of items to be stocked in the wholesale supply system based upon the forecast of retail and wholesale quantities and other information provided in the SSR. The method of support decision will be reflected by the assignment of an AAC. After assignment of the AAC, the integrated materiel manager will determine the projected support date and requirements to meet the level of support needed for the SSR. The date of support will be included in the response forwarded to the SSR submitter when the IMM date of support is different from the requested date of support. The integrated materiel manager will augment stocks as necessary to support the SSR requirement when sufficient funding is available.

    f. Make an annual comparison for the first 2 years after the date repair parts required (DRPR) of forecasted requirements to actual demands it receives for new items in its supply system. For those forecast requirements which actual demand varies from the forecast the integrated materiel manager will provide the SSR submitter with data showing the variances.

5. SSR PROCESSING

    a. <u>Military Department Submitter SSR Processing</u>. Upon receipt of an interim advice code transaction, the SSR submitter will review the ATC to determine proper response, update the item history record, and determine required actions. Actions may include conducting an engineering review, deleting original SSR, and preparing a new SSR. Specific actions include:

        (1) <u>Standard or Replacement Item</u>. SSR submitters will update their files to indicate that the standard and/or suitable replacement item is being supported in place of the item requested and will clear the follow-up suspense file for the support and NSN advice.

        (2) <u>Support for P/N Items</u>. SSR submitters will update their files to indicate existing NSN, assigned integrated materiel manager, substitute NSN, and support status for the item requested.

        (3) <u>P/N and/or CAGE Correction</u>. If the SSR submitter concurs with the corrected P/N and CAGE after engineering review, update files to reflect correct information. If the proposed corrections are not accepted, the SSR submitter will prepare an SSR delete action using type of change code (TOCC) D to delete the requirement and submit a new SSR using DIC W/CXB and RNJC 2.

        (4) <u>North American Treaty Organization (NATO) CAGE</u>. When the SSR submitter receives an interim response indicating the requested item of supply is manufactured in a foreign country, the interim response (ATC YH) will be posted to the SSR files, and the follow-up suspense timeframes will be adjusted to accommodate the additional 105 days from the date of the interim response.

        (5) <u>Offers</u>. SSR submitters will process offers and replies in accordance with timeframes contained in Table 6 of the appendix to this enclosure. SSR submitters will post the offer transaction to their SSR file and generate an output for technical review of the offer. An Offer Reply (DIC CX2) will be prepared and forwarded to the integrated materiel manager within 75 days of the date of advice (DADV) of the offered item.

        (6) <u>DCN</u>. DCNs are used to request changes to previously submitted SSRs. The SSR submitter will prepare an SSR with the appropriate TOCC to reflect changes to items that have been accepted or are being processed for support by the integrated materiel manager and are being deleted, superseded, or subjected to quantity changes by the user. These changes are normally the result of design or program changes, designated by TOCC P in the W/CWA Header. When support requirements are to be increased, TOCC C is used to reflect the revised quantity; items for which the support requirement of a Provisioning Control Code/Item Serial Number (PCC/ISN) is being reduced by the entire original requirement (and not superseded) will be processed as deletes (TOCC D). If the initial item request required a new NSN, that requirement is deleted. Deletes for partial quantities will be processed with TOCC H. Use CIC "V" for non-provisioning SSRs, indicated by a Type of Change Code (TOCC) "V" on the SSR, and use CIC "P" for provisioning SSRs, indicated by TOCC "N" on the SSR.

(7) <u>Passing Actions</u>. SSR submitters will process notice of the passing action to update their SSR files and to record the rerouting of the SSR. SSR submitters will also adjust the follow-up suspense on the basis of the advice date of the passing action and forward all follow-ups to the integrated materiel manager to whom the SSR was routed.

(8) <u>Offer Replies</u>. SSR submitters will prepare a reply to an offer within 75 days of the DADV of the offer to receive support. The ATC will indicate whether the SSR submitter accepts (ATC YM) or rejects (ATC YN) the offered item.

b. <u>IMM SSR Processing</u>. Integrated materiel managers will receive SSRs and validate for format. Controls will be established to ensure that advice is provided to the SSR submitter within allowed timeframes (see Enclosure 4 of this Volume). The following processing actions will be taken:

(1) <u>Initial and Change Transactions.</u> Initial and change transactions will be edited against control elements to ensure match conditions are met for changes and to prevent processing of duplicates. The SSRs will then be processed to determine if the item will be accepted for support, whether the item is under the cognizance of another manager and will be rerouted, or whether the SSR will be returned for validation, technical, or support reasons.

(2) <u>SSR Advice Transactions.</u> Appropriate SSR advice transactions will be prepared and forwarded to the SSR submitter to provide disposition of the SSR. Disposition action will be as follows:

(a) <u>Standard or Replacement Item</u>. Integrated materiel managers will support standard or replacement items instead of the item requested whenever the item requested is crossed to a standard or replacement item during provisioning screening or IEC. In addition to the standard or replacement NSN, the interim advice transaction (ATCs YJ, YR) will provide the item standardization code (ISC), phrase code (PC), and AAC of the replacing NSN. When forwarding the final advice to the SSR submitter, the integrated materiel manager will record the user against the substitute replacement NSN.

(b) <u>Requesting Support for P/N Items</u>. Integrated materiel managers will review the request and associated EDFP to determine whether the requested item will be supported or a standard, replacement, or substitute item will be offered. The CAGE and/or reference number will be reviewed and corrected, if possible, and the correction provided as an interim response, ATC YF, to the SSR submitter.

(3) <u>P/N and/or CAGE Correction</u>

(a) Integrated materiel managers may use EDFP and other DoD and/or industry sources to validate reference numbers and CAGEs contained in SSRs. The corrected CAGE or reference number or both are included in interim advice transactions (ATC YF). The integrated materiel manager will continue processing the correct item for support unless an SSR delete action (TOCC D) is received from the SSR submitter.

(b) An actual match includes P/Ns matched to NSNs during provisioning screening or in-house matches during IEC (actual or exact) where there is no discrepancy between the reference number category code (RNCC) or reference number variation code (RNVC) for the item requested in the SSR and the NSN to which the item is matched. The matched NSN should be included in interim advice transaction (ATC YG) and the integrated materiel manager will continue processing the matched NSN for support. SSRs that contain an RNJC will require the assignment of a new NSN.

(4) <u>NATO CAGE</u>. When the integrated materiel manager receives a CXB for an item produced in a foreign country, the integrated materiel manager will determine if a codification agreement exists with the country. If so, the integrated materiel manager will forward the request to the NATO National Codification Bureau (NCB) of the country, through the DLA Logistics Information System (DLIS), for NATO stock number assignment. The integrated materiel manager will forward an interim response (ATC YH) to the SSR submitter, informing the submitter that the request has been forwarded to the NATO NCB of the foreign country and notification of the NSN and the support advice will be received within 105 days.

(5) <u>Offers</u>

(a) The integrated materiel manager will submit offered NSN as interim response (ATC YL) with EDFP for offered NSN.

(b) Integrated materiel managers will forward offers of stock numbered items and P/N items to SSR submitters within 30 days of the SSR receipt. These offers will be identified by interim response (ATC YL/YQ). The integrated materiel manager will process offers and replies in accordance with timeframes contained in Table 6 of the appendix to this enclosure. If a reply (ATCs YM/YN) is not furnished to the integrated materiel manager within 75 days, the integrated materiel manager will cancel the SSR (ATC 08).

(c) When an integrated materiel manager is required to provide EDFP for a P/N item that is offered as a substitute, the SSR control elements (see Enclosure 4 of this Volume) corresponding to the requested item will be marked on the EDFP before forwarding the offer to the SSR submitter. This will be accomplished to ensure matchup of the offer and EDFP at the SSR submitter activity.

(d) Offer of reference number will be prepared under the procedures in Tables 3 through 17 of the appendix to this enclosure. The integrated materiel manager will submit offered reference number as interim response (ATC YQ) with EDFP for offered reference number.

(6) <u>Passing Actions</u>. Integrated materiel managers will:

(a) Determine through provisioning screening if an NSN is currently being managed by another integrated materiel manager. The integrated materiel manager that originally received the SSR will pass it to the managing integrated materiel manager and provide passing action advice to the original submitter. The originally submitted SSR will be revised by placing an "R" in position 6 of the header (DIC CWA), which identifies the fact that the SSR has been passed, and by changing the activity code, positions 4-5, to the activity code of the managing integrated materiel manager, and will be transmitted electronically. Passing action advice will be provided by electronic transmission to the original submitter with an ATC YK and the activity code of the managing activity in positions 75-76.

(b) Pass the SSR to the correct integrated materiel manager when it is determined that the item requested should be classified in a Federal Supply Class (FSC) managed by that integrated materiel manager. The integrated materiel manager that originally received the SSR will record the rationale for re-identifying the FSC. The integrated materiel manager will then forward the form and all technical data received with the originally submitted line item supply support request (LISSR) to the managing integrated materiel manager with the activity code, positions 4-5, revised to reflect the correct integrated materiel manager activity and an "R" in position 6 of DIC CWA. Passing action advice will be provided by electronic transmission to the original submitter with ATC YC, and activity code of the correct integrated materiel manager activity in positions 75-76, and the FSC in positions 77-80. SSRs will only be passed by an integrated materiel manager to another integrated materiel manager one time; if the integrated materiel manager receiving a passed SSR determines that yet another integrated materiel manager is the appropriate manager, then the integrated materiel manager will obtain an NSN and assume management of item in recommended FSC and subsequently take appropriate action to reclassify to correct FSC. Integrated materiel managers will forward EDFP to another integrated materiel manager when passing the SSR.

(c) Return the SSR to the SSR submitter when it is determined that the item is not appropriate for integrated materiel manager management.

(d) Record the passing action in the SSR files to provide a record of action taken.

(7) Offer Replies. Integrated materiel managers will:

(a) Post the offer reply to their SSR files and clear the follow-up suspense. If the offer is accepted, the integrated materiel manager will generate file maintenance, catalog, and inventory control actions to support the offered item. If the accepted offer is a P/N item, the integrated materiel manager will obtain and provide an NSN for the item. If the offered item is an NSN, the requested P/N will be added as an additional reference number (within 30 days of the acceptance).

(b) If the offered item is not acceptable to the SSR submitter, the integrated materiel manager will initiate action to support the requested item. The integrated materiel manager will provide final advice on the SSR within the allowed timeframes based upon the date of the offer reply rather than the DOR.

(8) Budgeting and Funding. The integrated materiel manager will budget for and fund provisioning requirements for items that are recorded as stocked in the integrated materiel manager's distribution system. The integrated materiel manager will procure retail quantities of

centrally procured non-stocked items that do not possess a weapon system designator code (WSDC) and an appropriate essentiality code only upon receipt of a funded requisition.

(9) SSR Validation Process. The integrated materiel manager may validate SSRs that have a total dollar value of $2500 or more. If validation is appropriate, the integrated materiel manager will contact the SSR submitter electronically, a procurement lead time plus 60 days prior to the SSR support date. The submitter will be allowed 30 days to respond to the validation request. A follow-up request will be sent after the initial request if no response is received. The submitter will be allowed 14 days to respond to the follow-up request. Retail and wholesale quantities will be adjusted according to the validated response or quantities will be deleted if no response is received. This data will be maintained by the integrated materiel manager for a 3-year period.

c. Military Department IMM SSR Processing. Military Department integrated materiel manager will:

(1) Return the SSR to the SSR submitter when it is determined that the item is not appropriate for management by that integrated materiel manager.

(2) Record the SSR in their files to provide a record of action taken.

6. SSR REJECT AND FOLLOW-UP ADVICE PROCEDURES. SSR rejects and follow-up advices are received by the original submitter and processed accordingly.

a. SSR Submitter Advice Procedures

(1) Rejects

(a) Rejected SSRs will be researched to determine disposition (i.e., cancellation, correction, or resubmission). All corrected and resubmitted SSRs will contain the same control elements as the rejected SSRs, except for the DOR.

(b) SSR submitters will post rejects to their SSR files and take appropriate corrective action. The SSR files will be updated to clear any follow-up suspense and to record the item as complete.

(c) SSR submitters may initiate action to support the item as a retained item or request support for commodities such as fuels or clothing under the special procedures applicable to these categories of items.

(2) Follow-up and Responses

(a) SSR submitters will generate follow-ups (DIC CX3) in accordance with Table 16 of the appendix to this enclosure. Additional follow-ups may be sent at 20-day intervals until the integrated materiel manager responds.

(b) Upon receipt of a follow-up, SSR submitters will expedite review and respond to the offer. If the SSR submitter receives an ATC 08 from the integrated materiel manager, a new SSR will be required.

b. <u>IMM SSR Advice Procedures</u>

(1) <u>Rejects</u>. SSRs may be rejected for edit/validation, duplicate, technical, support, or other reasons. The reason for rejection will be defined by the returned ATC and comments. The integrated materiel manager will maintain a record of rejected transactions in the SSR files in order to respond to follow-ups.

(a) <u>Invalid Data Conditions</u>. Integrated materiel managers will process all SSR transactions through the edit/validation procedures and criteria. Invalid data conditions will be identified by the applicable ATCs, and rejected SSRs will be posted to the SSR files prior to forwarding to the SSR submitter.

(b) <u>Duplicate SSRs</u>. Duplicate SSRs will be rejected by the receiving integrated materiel manager using an ATC 42. Resubmitted SSRs and follow-up suspense dates in the SSR files will be adjusted to reflect the new DOR to prevent rejection due to duplicated control elements.

(c) <u>Unmatched Conditions</u>. Unlike duplicate SSRs, changes to SSR replies to offers and follow-ups will reflect the same values in the control elements, including DOR, of the original SSR. SSRs with unmatched conditions will be rejected by receiving integrated materiel manager using an ATC 58 or 66.

(d) <u>Technical Rejects</u>. Integrated materiel managers will reject SSRs for technical reasons when the SSR includes CAGE and/or reference numbers that cannot be corrected, non-definitive UI, or lack of other EDFP required for assigning an NSN or procuring an item. The ATC identifies the specific reject condition.

(e) <u>Incorrect Manager Rejects</u>. Integrated materiel managers will return SSRs that are not accepted for support because the items do not fall within the cognizance of the integrated materiel manager and cannot be rerouted to another manager. Included within this category are such conditions as items that should be coded for service retention or are in a class of items that do not come under the SSR procedures. The ATC contained in the reject identifies the reject condition.

(f) <u>Other Rejects</u>. Integrated materiel managers will use ATC 36 only when no other reject ATC applies and additional information is required to explain the reject condition. This reject permits exception data to be entered into the advice transaction instead of being provided manually. The reason for the reject will be entered into the remarks block of the DIC CX5. This permits the explanatory information to be sent electronically and avoids the need to match explanatory information sent by mail with the reject transaction which is sent electronically. The

DIC CX5 will be used only for reject advice – not offers, acceptances of standard, or substitute items – and only when ATC 36 applies.

   (2) Follow-up and Responses

      (a) Follow-up for Advice. Integrated materiel managers will match the follow-up received from SSR submitters against their SSR files and the green product requirements. If the follow-up does not match a request with the same SSR control elements, a DIC CX4 with ATC 66 will be prepared and forwarded to the SSR submitter within 15 days of the follow-up date. If advice has already been provided, an image of the advice with a current date will be provided to the SSR submitter on a DIC CX4. If the SSR is recorded on the files and advice has not been provided, a DIC CX4 with ATC YY will be forwarded to the SSR submitter. An appropriate advice response will be provided within 15 days of the date of last follow-up from the SSR submitter.

      (b) Follow-up for Offer Reply. Integrated materiel managers will send a follow-up, DIC CX1 with ATC YZ, after 55 days from the date of the original offer if a reply has not been received. If a response is not received from the SSR submitter within 75 days of the date of the offer, the integrated materiel manager will reject support for the item using an ATC 08.

   (3) Follow-up Suspense Files. The integrated materiel manager SSR files will be updated to clear follow-up suspense files and to record the item as complete.

7. SSR FINAL ADVICE PROCEDURES. Final advice received when the SSR action has been completed is based on the AAC assigned to the NSN.

   a. IMM Positive Final Advice. Integrated materiel managers will forward, when the request for support has been processed, a positive final advice, identified by ATC YA, YB, YD, YE, or YX, to the SSR submitter. The NSN for which support has been accepted is shown in positions 8-20. The AAC for that NSN is shown in position 30. If the ATC is YX, the date upon which the integrated materiel manager can accept support for the NSN is shown in positions 77-80.

   b. SSR Submitters Positive Final Advice. SSR submitters will receive the positive advice and update their SSR files to indicate that the item requested has been accepted by the integrated materiel manager and to close out that SSR. If the item requested was a P/N the files will be updated to record the NSN and to close out that SSR. If an ATC YX is received by the SSR submitter and materiel is required prior to the date reflected on the ATC YX, the SSR submitter may initiate procurement for that quantity of materiel required to support operational equipment until the IMM support date.

8. NOTIFICATION OF REPETITIVE DEMANDS FOR NONREGISTERED PARTICIPANTS. Repetitive demands occur when two or more requisitions are recorded within a 180-day period on NSNs or P/N items where the participant is not a recorded user.

a. Participants will be notified via electronic transmission or listings after items are requisitioned of all items for which an NSN assignment has been accomplished. Points of contact for receipt of notifications are located in Table 21 of the appendix to this enclosure.

b. Upon receipt of the notification, the participant will identify user registration or NSN assignment requirements to the integrated materiel manager via SSRs. No user registration or NSN assignment will be accomplished by the integrated materiel manager based on repetitive demand.

c. Integrated materiel managers will record the applicable countries on items requisitioned in support of foreign military sales (FMS) cases. The integrated materiel managers will apply the appropriate major organizational entity (MOE) rules reflecting the individual country's interest on the item requisitioned in support of FMS cases.

d. Integrated materiel managers will identify repetitive demand on NSN and P/N items on which a participant is not recorded as a user and will initiate notification to participants for appropriate action. Requisitions for P/N items are authorized to be submitted to DLA and/or GSA from overseas military activities only. All others should submit such requisitions to their parent Service. Integrated materiel managers will prepare the notification as outlined in Tables 22 and 23 of the appendix to this enclosure.

e. Participants will:

(1) Initiate review of notifications received from integrated materiel manager.

(2) Effect necessary contact with appropriate activities in conducting review and investigation of the NSN and P/N items requisitioned.

(3) Initiate action to record the Service FMS sponsorship (record), if applicable.

(4) Prepare and submit an SSR for NSN assignment or user registration if review supports continued authorized use of the item.

(5) Provide notification of unauthorized items to the requisitioner to prevent future erroneous requisitioning.

APPENDIX TO ENCLOSURE 3

SSR ATCS

Table 1. SSR ATC – Alphabetic

CODE	DESCRIPTION
YA	Final Acceptance. The item will be centrally managed, stocked, and issued (AAC D or G only) and the requirement will be supported by the DRPR. The assigned NSN is identified in positions 8-20.
YB	Final Acceptance. The item will be managed as a local purchase item (AAC L) or direct order from a central contract/schedule (AAC I). The NSN under which support will be furnished is identified in positions 8-20.
YC	Interim Advice. Passing action. The P/N submitted is classified to a FSC which is managed by another integrated materiel manager. The SSR and any EDFP furnished have been forwarded to the appropriate integrated materiel manager. Update SSR submitter files and expect a final advice within 75 days of the DADV in positions 53-56 from the integrated materiel manager identified in positions 75-76. The applicable FSC is provided in positions 77-80.
YD	Final Acceptance. The item will be managed as direct delivery under a central contract (AAC H) or centrally procured but not stocked (AAC J). The NSN under which support will be furnished is identified in positions 8-20.
YE	Final Acceptance. The item will be managed as an insurance/numeric stockage objective item (AAC Z) and the requirement will be supported by the DRPR. The NSN under which support will be furnished is identified in positions 8-20.
YF	Interim Advice. The P/N or CAGE code or both submitted on the SSR is in error. Correct P/N and CAGE are provided in positions 8-39 and 60-64, respectively. The item is continuing to be processed with the corrected data. A final advice will be provided within 35 days of the date of this interim advice. If the correction is not acceptable, resubmit the SSR with a TOCC D and prepare a new SSR with RNJC 2.
YG	Interim Advice. The item submitted on the SSR without NSN or RNJC had an actual match in the FLIS database. The matched NSN is reflected in positions 8-20 of this line item advice transaction (LIAT). The SSR is continuing to be processed with the NSN in positions 8-20. A final advice will be provided within 35 days of the date of the CX1 interim advice. If the item shown in positions 8-20 is not acceptable, resubmit the SSR with a TOCC D and prepare a new SSR with an appropriate RNJC.
YH	Interim Advice. The P/N and/or CAGE code submitted on the SSR identifies an item manufactured in a foreign country. A request for NSN assignment has been forwarded to the NATO NCB of the manufacturing country, through DLIS. A final advice will be provided within 105 days of the date of CX1 interim advice.

Table 1. SSR ATC – Alphabetic, Continued

CODE	DESCRIPTION
YJ	<u>Interim Advice</u>. The NSN submitted is identified as "cancelled-replaced by" or "cancelled duplicate of" in the FLIS database and will not be supported. The NSN in positions 8-20 of this LIAT is the superseding NSN. The SSR is continuing to be processed with the superseding NSN. A final advice will be provided within 35 days of the CXI interim advice. If the item shown in positions 8-20 is not acceptable, resubmit the original SSR with TOCC D and determine own method of support for the superseded item.
YK	<u>Interim Advice</u>. The NSN requested has been identified in the FLIS database as being managed by another integrated materiel manager. The SSR has been forwarded as of the date of this advice. Final advice may be expected from the integrated materiel manager reflected in cc 75-76 within 25 days after the date in positions 53-56. NSNs managed by a Service integrated materiel manager will be rejected with ATC 63.
YL	<u>Offer</u>. The NSN in positions 8-20 identifies an item currently managed by the integrated materiel manager and is offered as an alternate or substitute item in lieu of the item requested on the originally submitted SSR. The item requested is identified as a possible, probable, or associated match in the FLIS database or has been identified by this integrated materiel manager during IEC. Acceptance of the offer with an ATC YM will establish the requested item as an advisory reference to the offered item if not already identified to the offered item in the FLIS database. A reply by the SSR submitter to this offer is mandatory. The integrated materiel manager will provide a final advice of ATC YA, YB, YD, YE, or YX upon receipt of the acceptance reply with an ATC YM from the submitter. Rejection of the offered item with an ATC YN will reinstate the request for the original item. Failure to reply will create automatic follow-up transactions with an ATC YZ in 55 days. Failure to provide an ATC YM or YN reply within 75 days from the date of offer will result in an ATC 08 rejecting the originally submitted SSR. Subsequent resubmission after receipt of the ATC 08 advice will require submittal of a new SSR under a new DOR. The resubmission of the SSR will be provided on a DIC CXA when the offered NSN is acceptable. Whenever the offered NSN is not accepted and resubmission of the originally requested P/N is required, the resubmission of the SSR will be accomplished by submitting a DIC CXB with an appropriate RNJC.
YM	<u>Response</u>. SSR submitter to integrated materiel manager only - the NSN or P/N and CAGE code offered under ATC YL/YQ respectively for the ISN (MN) in positions 43-48 is acceptable.
YN	<u>Response</u>. SSR submitter to integrated materiel manager only - the NSN or P/N and CAGE code offered under ATC YL/YQ respectively in positions 43-48 is not acceptable. The item identified in the original SSR is required. The SSR submitter will return all technical data provided with YL/YQ offer to the integrated materiel manager for YN responses and cite differentiating characteristics where applicable.

Table 1. SSR ATC – Alphabetic, Continued

CODE	DESCRIPTION
YQ	The reference number in positions 8-39 and the CAGE code in 60-64 identify a non-NSN item offered as an alternate or substitute. A reply by the SSR submitter to this offer is mandatory. The integrated materiel manager will provide a final advice of ATC YA, YB, YD, YE, or YX upon receipt of the acceptance reply with an ATC YM from the submitter. A rejection of the offered item with an ATC YN will reinstate the request for the original item. Failure to reply will create automatic follow-up transactions with ATC YZ in 55 days. Failure to provide an ATC YM or YN reply within 75 days from the date of offer will result in an ATC 08 rejecting the originally submitted SSR. Subsequent resubmission after receipt of the ATC 08 advice will require submittal of a new SSR under a new DOR. The re-submittal should identify the offered P/N if it is acceptable. If the original P/N is required and the alternate or substitute is unacceptable, the appropriate RNJC will be used in the SSR.
YR	Interim Advice. The NSN submitted is identified as being nonstandard in the FLIS database as the result of a coordinated standardization action and will not be supported. The NSN in positions 8-20 of this LIAT identifies the standard item. If the item shown in positions 8-20 is not acceptable, resubmit the original SSR with a TOCC D and determine own method of support for the nonstandard item. The SSR is continuing to be processed with the standard item. A final advice will be provided within 35 days of the date of the DIC CX1 interim advice.
YT	Interim Advice. Other than 5 numerics are contained in positions 25-29 (retail quantity) and/or 32-36 (wholesale quantity) of the LISSR. Invalid entries were overlaid with zeros and the SSR is continuing to be processed. If quantitative requirements exist for this item, submit a TOCC C document with valid entries in positions 25-29 and/or 32-36. A final advice will be provided within 35 days of the date of the DIC CX 1 interim advice.
YX	Final Acceptance. Integrated materiel manager to SSR submitter only - the DRPR (positions 25-28, PDSSR) has passed or was less than the procurement lead time identified in positions 43-48. Procurement action initiated after the requirement date for the NSN in positions 8-20 will be supported by the date indicated in positions 77-80. If the new support date in positions 77-80 is not acceptable, the requiring activity may procure the retail quantity necessary for initial support of the equipment being introduced to cover the time until the integrated materiel manager will be in a support position. The AAC in position 30 indicates the method of management assigned the NSN. ATC YX will not be used in reply to Condition 1 SSRs for items currently managed and stocked by integrated materiel managers. This ATC is not used by Service integrated materiel manager to respond to SSR submitter.
YY	Interim Advice. Final supply support determination is pending. Decisions will be provided within 15 days.
YZ	Follow-up. This notice is provided by an integrated materiel manager as a 55-day follow-up to an item awaiting a response from the SSR submitter to a previously furnished ATC YL or YQ. The original SSR will be rejected with ATC 08 if no reply is received within 75 days of the date of offer.

Table 2. SSR ATC - Numeric

CODE	DESCRIPTION
02	P/N and CAGE code identifies a military drawing which was not submitted with the SSR. Support is rejected.
03	Integrated materiel manager (DLA and/or GSA) to SSR submitter only - the NSN or P/N is tentatively classified in an FSC excluded from IMC. The applicable FSC appears in positions 8-11. Support is rejected.
04	UI in positions 53-54 is invalid, blank, or different from established UI for currently managed integrated materiel manager NSN and cannot be converted to an equal definitive UI. Support is rejected.
07	Integrated materiel manager (DLA and/or GSA) to SSR submitter only - the item submitted in the SSR does not contain a unit price (U/P) in 74-80 of the LISSR or the U/P contains other than numerics. Support is rejected.
08	The submitting activity has failed to respond to the integrated materiel manager offer of a standard/alternate/substitute item (YL/YQ) within 75 days of offer. Support is rejected. The receipt of an ATC 08 by the SSR submitter will require the SSR submitter to submit a new SSR. If accepting the offered item, the SSR submitter will be required to also submit a cataloging add reference transaction (DIC LAR) to the appropriate integrated materiel manager for submission to DLIS to add the originally submitted part/reference number to the accepted alternate item NSN.
09	Integrated materiel manager (DLA and/or GSA) to SSR submitter only – the item will not be supported because data provided is inadequate for minimum reference type cataloging identification. Resubmit under a new DOR assuring that all data required are provided. Minimum data for cataloging purposes are CAGE code, P/N, and item name. In the absence of item identifying technical data, the item name must be furnished via DIC CXF. Support is rejected.
11	The item requested does not fall within the cognizance of the SSR procedures. Such commodities as fuel, subsistence, clothing, and textiles are covered by special procedures. Required items should be processed under the specific regulations governing these commodities. Support is rejected.
12	The AMC indicates restrictive procurement. Justification or EDFP was not received. Submitter should resubmit SSR with required data or, if the AMC was invalid, with the correct AMC. Support is rejected.
13	The CAGE code submitted on the SSR is missing or in error and the integrated materiel manager is unable to correct. Support is rejected.
14	The P/N submitted on the SSR is missing or in error and the integrated materiel manager is unable to correct. Support is rejected.
18	Integrated materiel manager (DLA and/or GSA) to SSR submitter only - the source code in positions 4 I-42 of the LISSR is invalid. Support is rejected.
19	The P/N and CAGE code submitted on the SSR are missing or in error and the integrated materiel manager is unable to correct. Support is rejected.

Table 2. SSR ATC – Numeric, Continued

CODE	DESCRIPTION
20	The manufacturer identified in the original LISSR advises the P/N is non-procurable or unidentifiable. Attempts to obtain other sources of supply have been unsuccessful. Support is rejected.
21	The P/N/CAGE code for this ISN is not compatible with the technical data submitted for the same ISN. Support is rejected.
28	The NSN in positions 8-20 of W/CXA LISSR contains other than 13 numeric characters. Support is rejected.
31	P/N LISSR received with missing CXB transactions 1 or 2. Support is rejected
32	The LISSR cannot be processed because mandatory data are missing or incomplete. Support is rejected.
34	Item submitted without NSN or RNJC is a possible, probable, or associated match in the FLIS database and cannot be processed. Matched NSN is shown in positions 8-20. Support is rejected.
36	SSR returned for reason not covered by existing ATC. Specific reason for return is provided by CX5. Support is rejected.
38	Integrated materiel manager (DLA/GSA) to SSR submitter only. Production lead time (PLT) is blank or other than numerics. Support is rejected.
40	Shelf Life code in positions 71 is blank or invalid. Support is rejected.
42	Duplicate SSRs with the same control elements have been received. The first SSR has been processed by the integrated materiel manager. If an additional requirement exists, submit a new SSR with the appropriate TOCC. Support is rejected.
43	Integrated materiel manager (DLA/GSA) to SSR submitter only. Demilitarization code in positions 56 is blank or other than A through N (except I). Support is rejected.
44	Technical data was not submitted and date technical data to be supplied (DTDS) in positions 69-72 or technical data justification code (TDJC) in positions 73 was blank or invalid. Resubmit the SSR with the technical data or with appropriate coding. Support is rejected.
45	Integrated materiel manager (DLA and/or GSA) to SSR submitter only - item submitted is identified as AAC F (fabricate or assemble), T (condemned), or W (generic item) and cannot be supported.
58	SSR change request unmatched to previous submission. Support is rejected.
59	Service integrated materiel manager to SSR submitter only - missing or MOE rule. Support is rejected.
62	Integrated Materiel Manager (Service) to SSR submitter only - the item has no replacement, wholesale stocks are exhausted, no future procurement planned. Support is rejected. If item is still required, recommend integrated materiel manager reassignment action be initiated.
63	The item is managed by NSA, DTRA, or Tank-automotive and Armaments Command; or the NSN is being managed by a Service. Support is rejected.

Table 2. SSR ATC – Numeric, Continued

CODE	DESCRIPTION
65	The NSN submitted is not recorded in the FLIS database and will not be supported. Review background of the NSN entry into the DoD supply system and accomplish IMC under the procedures contained in Volume 3 of this Manual. If this NSN is in error, resubmit the correct NSN with a new DOR.
66	No record of this SSR exists at this integrated materiel manager. Support is rejected.
68	FLIS future data indicates condition adverse to supply support, e.g., NSN cancelled (without replacement), LR or FSC change is pending. Support is rejected. If requirement still exists, resubmit SSR with appropriate NSN after effective date of change.
70	LISSR contains non-definitive UI and technical data furnishing quantitative measure, count, or composition was not received. Support is rejected. Resubmit new SSR with supporting data quantifying the UI.
71	NSN is cancelled, inactive, or terminal without replacement in the FLIS database and cannot be reinstated. Support is rejected

Table 3. SSR Data Elements

DATA ELEMENT CODE	DATA ELEMENT DESCRIPTION
AAC	A code denoting how, as distinguished from where and under what restrictions, an item will be acquired. (See Table 58 of Chapter 3 of Volume 10 of Reference (f).)
Activity Code	A two-character alphanumeric code assigned for activity identification. Activity code to (ACT) is the activity to which the SSR is sent. Activity code from (ACF) is the activity from which the SSR is sent. (See Part 4 of Table 104 of Chapter 3 of Volume 10 of Reference (f).)
Additional Reference Number	Any additional number which identifies the same item of production or supply as the primary manufacturer's part number or NSN.
AMC	A one-character numeric code reflecting the decision of the SSR submitter as to technique of purchasing to be employed from a planned procurement review. (See Table 71 of Volume 10 of Reference (f).
AMSC	A one-digit alphanumeric code which provides information concerning the status of technical documentation. (See Table 71 of Volume 10 of Reference (f).)
Conditions	Conditions prescribe the status of supply management and identification of items in order to prescribe the minimum data needed by the integrated materiel manager to assume management and/or provide additional support for items already managed.

Table 3. SSR Data Elements, Continued

DATA ELEMENT CODE	DATA ELEMENT DESCRIPTION
Condition 1	The SSR submitter is requesting supply support for an item with NSN assigned centrally managed by an integrated materiel manager. IMC to integrated materiel manager DLA and/or GSA required if not previously coded by submitting SSR submitter service. Integrated materiel manager-managed items classified for central procurement but not stocked (AAC J), may be included in this condition when the SSR submitter considers that the provisioning requirement justifies reclassifying the item to centrally managed and stocked.
Condition 2	SSR submitter is requesting support for an item with an NSN and neither the SSR submitter nor another DoD activity is currently recorded in the FLIS database as manager(s) of the item request. The item is not currently managed by the receiving integrated materiel manager.
Condition 3	SSR submitter is requesting support for an item without an NSN and being IMC to the integrated materiel manager (DLA and/or GSA) for management, including cataloging and supply support. Also, an SSR submitter is requesting support for an item without an NSN under joint Military Department provisioning wherein the procuring agency exercises Service IMM responsibility for P/N items for management and cataloging actions.
Contract/Control Number	A number, 20 characters or less, of numeric or alpha-numeric configuration, which identifies the procurement document on which the end item is being purchased. The originator may use, in lieu of the procurement documents, registry number, allowance list number, or any significant number not exceeding 20 characters which is used to control the project in-house.
DADV	The date on which the LIAC is produced by the integrated materiel manager to the SSR submitter, or a response is sent from the SSR submitter to an integrated materiel manager.
Date NSNs Required	The latest date that NSNs will be needed by the SSR submitter for allowance lists or other document preparation. To be filled in only when NSNs are required in less than 60 days after receipt of the request by the integrated materiel manager.
Date Support will be Provided	Date that stock will be available in the integrated materiel manager's supply system for requisitioning because the procurement lead time exceeds the time between receipt of the LISSR and the DRPR.
Dates	Dates used in SSRs are four-character numeric fields constructed by placing the last digit of the calendar year in the first position, and the numeric day of the calendar year in the next three positions to the right. For example, the 31st of January 2008 is expressed as 8031, and the 1st of February 2008 is expressed as 8032.

Table 3. SSR Data Elements, Continued

DATA ELEMENT CODE	DATA ELEMENT DESCRIPTION
Demilitarization Codes	A table of codes instructing the user on method and degree of demilitarizing items when required. (See Table 38 of Chapter 3 of Volume 10 of Reference (f).)
DIC	The DICs are three-character alphanumeric codes that identify SSR transactions, and are constructed and defined as follows: 　a. The first position (Column 1) is a fixed alphabetic character: C if action is to an integrated materiel manager (DLA and/or GSA); W if action is to a Service integrated materiel manager. 　b. The second position (Column 2) is a variable alphabetic character (W, X) and identifies various formats. 　c. The third position (Column 3) is a variable alpha or numeric character and identifies the data being transmitted relative to format. Numerics in the third position identify advice format. 　d. Use and definitions of the codes are: 　　(1) W/CWA - identifies the transmission of provisioning or program data via PDSSR. 　　(2) The following codes are used on LISSRS: 　　　(a) W/CXA - Identifies an SSR with an NSN. 　　　(b) W/CXB – Identifies an SSR with a manufacturer's P/N. ((Service)/SSR submitter transactions under Joint Services Provisioning.) (DIC WXB applies to IMM) 　　　(c) CXG – Identifies an additional reference number to CX-CXB, or CXC SSRs. (Not used in SSR submission to Service integrated materiel manager.) 　　　(d) CXK – Identifies an additional user on a multi-Service contract wherein the contracting Service by agreement is the principal and other claimants are additional users. The principal submits SSRs for total requirements of all claimants and prepares user transactions for each claimant to accomplish IMC and registration of user interest. (Not used in SSR submission to Service integrated materiel manager.) 　　(3) These DICS indicate line item advice code (LIACs): 　　　(a) CX1 - Identifies advice being provided to the SSR submitter regarding a specific SSR. A LIAC is required to be sent for each LISSR received. 　　　(b) CX2 - Identifies advice being provided by SSR submitter in reply to YL/YQ advice furnished by the integrated materiel manager under CX1. 　　　(c) CX3 -SSR submitter follow-up on a LISSR for which initial or final advice is overdue. 　　　(d) CX4 - integrated materiel manager response to CX3 SSR submitter follow-up. 　　　(e) CX5 - Identifies reasons for return of SSRs not covered

Table 3. SSR Data Elements, Continued

DATA ELEMENT CODE	DATA ELEMENT DESCRIPTION
	by existing ATC. (f) CXT - Identifies quality requirements for an item being provisioned.
Document Availability Code	An alphanumeric code indicating the current status of technical documentation availability. (See Table 5 of Chapter 3 of Volume 10 of Reference (f).)
DOR	The date on which the SSRs are sent from the SSR submitter to the integrated materiel manager. Except for TOCC N (new submission), the DOR in the original submission will be repeated in all subsequent submissions (involving changes) pertaining to the same PCC and ISN. SSRs which were previously rejected and require resubmission, must be assigned a new DOR for the new submission. The DOR will not be more than 15 days before the date of receipt by the integrated materiel manager.
DRPR	The date that material must be in the integrated materiel manager's supply system to support requisitions submitted by principal (SSR submitter's Service) user of the end item.
DTDS	Date that technical data is to be supplied to the integrated materiel manager for Condition 3 SSRS initially submitted transactions. The date on which technical data are to be without technical data not used in IMM.
End Item Name, Type, or Model Number	The name, model number, or type designation of the end item being supported. Use noun and modifiers abbreviated as necessary. The legend is 13 characters, alphabetic or alphanumeric, and is intended to identify the end item by noun and modifiers (abbreviated), type number (if assigned), and model number (if assigned).
End Item Quantity	A five-digit number which denotes the quantity of end items to be supported by the SSRS sent to an integrated materiel manager. The number of end items is entered from right to left and unused spaces filled with zeros. If quantity of end items is more than 99999, indicate 99999, the maximum number permitted by the form.

Table 3. SSR Data Elements, Continued

DATA ELEMENT CODE	DATA ELEMENT DESCRIPTION
Engineering Data for Provisioning (EDFP)	Technical data which provides definitive identification of dimensional, material, mechanical, electrical, functional and/or other characteristics that depict the physical characteristics, location, and function of the item. It includes specifications, standards, drawings, photographs, descriptions, assembly and general arrangement drawings, schematic diagrams, wiring, cabling diagrams, and similar data needed to indicate the location and functions of the item. EDFP augments the SSR by providing additional information necessary to identify, classify, and characterize an item of supply. EDFP has also been referred to as supplementary provisioning technical data (SPTD) and engineering data for provisioning (EDFP), all of which are referred to in section 2320 of title 10, United States Code (Reference (i)), and subpart 227.7102-1 of Reference (h) as form, fit, and function data.
Essentiality Code (EC)	A one-digit numeric code indicating the degree to which the failure of the part affects the ability of the end item to perform its intended operation. The codes are: a. 1 - Failure to this part will render the item inoperable. b. 3 - Failure to this part will not render the end item inoperable. c. 5 - Item does not qualify for the assignment of code 1 but is needed for personal safety. d. 6 - Item does not qualify for assignment of code 1 but is needed for legal, climatic, or other requirements peculiar to the planned operational environment of the end item. e. 7 - Item does not qualify for assignment of code 1 but is needed to prevent impairment of or the temporary reduction of operational effectiveness of the end item.
Executive Service	That Service which is formally designated, assigned responsibility, and delegated authority for life-cycle management for a multi-Service system or equipment jointly used by two or more Military Departments.

Table 3. SSR Data Elements, Continued

DATA ELEMENT CODE	DATA ELEMENT DESCRIPTION
Interchangeability Code	A two-character, alphabetic code to indicate interchangeability when an item previously requested is being replaced by a new item because of a design or other change. This code is inserted in the applicable TOCC R and S transactions to signify the interchangeability between the original item and the replacement item. The codes to be used are: a. OW – This code signifies one-way interchangeability as follows: 1. When used on the transaction which describes changes to the original item (TOCC R), means that the original item may be used until exhausted. 2. When used on the transaction which submits the replacement items (TOCC S), OW means that the new item may be used to replace the original item. b. TW – This code signifies that the old and new items are interchangeable with each other and appears in both (TOCC R and S) transactions. c. NI – This code signifies that items are not interchangeable: 1. When used on the transaction which describes changes to the original item (TOCC R), NI means that item is not interchangeable with the replacement item (TOCC S). 2. When used on the transaction which submits the replacement item (TOCC S), NI means that there placement item is not interchangeable with the original item. d. OM – This code is used on the transaction which describes changes to the original item. It signifies that the old item (TOCC R) is interchangeable with the new item (TOCC S) only if modified to the new item configuration and only in the new item application. e. IM – This code is used on the transaction which describes changes to the original item. It signifies that the old item (TOCC R) is interchangeable in both the old and new application only if modified to the new item (TOCC S) configuration.
ISN	A number not to exceed six characters used for sequential line item control and for means of communication control. This legend may be alphabetic, numeric, or alphanumeric, e.g., PL index number. The serial number assigned in this legend must be repeated in the serial number legends of all LIACs for the same item and all transactions generated by any subsequent actions which pertain to the same line item under the same PCC including any succeeding design or program changes. In lieu of sequentially assigned serial numbers, the originator may enter a six-character number used locally by the originator for sequential control and reference. Serial number with more than six characters cannot be used.

Table 3. SSR Data Elements, Continued

DATA ELEMENT CODE	DATA ELEMENT DESCRIPTION
Item IMC	As defined in Volume 1 of this Manual, this code is mandatory for any item being submitted without an NSN and for any item with an NSN not previously coded for integrated management by the submitting Service. IMC is not required in SSRs from SSR submitter to a Service integrated materiel manager.
Item Name	The basic noun name and adjective modifiers of the item of supply. The kinds of item names are: (1) approved item name (published in Cataloging Handbook H6, Federal Item Name Directory for Supply Cataloging, Section A, Alphabetic Index of Names), and (2) part name (applied to the item by a Government activity or by a manufacturer when no approved item name exists). The use of the approved item name from cataloging handbook H6 is preferable. The name legend provides for 35 characters in positions 8-42 but the item name may overrun for an additional 12 characters into positions 69–80 as necessary. Item name and adjective modifiers are alphanumeric, with a maximum length of characters.
LIAC	Designated to provide essential advice data on SSRs submitted. integrated materiel managers used to offer preferred items in lieu of a nonstandard or new item requested or advise the SSR submitter of any specific item accepted, not accepted, or accepted conditionally and reasons therefore, or advise the SSR submitter of the NSN assigned to a new item.
LISSR	Contains supply and EDFP relative to individual items required, SSR submitters furnish initial supply and provisioning data and changes there to supporting integrated materiel managers for each line item for which support is requested.

Table 3. SSR Data Elements, Continued

DATA ELEMENT CODE	DATA ELEMENT DESCRIPTION
Maintenance Code	A two-digit code which indicates the lowest maintenance echelon authorized to use (first position) and completely repair (second position) support items. The codes (shown generally ascending from lowest to highest echelons of maintenance) are: a. First position Code Explanation C Crew or operator authorized to remove/replace the item. O Support item is removed, replaced, used at the direct F support echelon of maintenance. Support item is removed, replaced, and used at the direct support echelon of maintenance. H Support item is removed, replaced, and used at the general support echelon of maintenance. L Support item is removed, replaced, and used at the designated specialized repair activity. D Support item is removed, replaced, and used at depot only. b. Second position Code Explanation O The lowest maintenance echelon capable of complete repair of the support item is the organizational echelon. F The lowest maintenance echelon capable of repair of the support item is the direct support echelon. H The lowest maintenance echelon capable of repair of the support item is the general support echelon. L The lowest activity capable of complete repair of the support item is special repair activity. D The lowest maintenance echelon capable of complete repair of the support item is the depot echelon. Z Non-repairable. No repair is authorized. B The item may be reconditioned by adjusting, lubricating, etc., at the user level. No parts or special tools are procured for the maintenance of this item.

Table 3. SSR Data Elements, Continued

DATA ELEMENT CODE	DATA ELEMENT DESCRIPTION
Manufacturer's Part Number/Reference number	This field legend in the LISSR is intended to include any combination of alphanumeric which completely identifies a single design item or item of production which identifies the item of supply concept of the requiring activity for the application in which the item will be used. The number may be a part, drawing, or catalog number of the actual manufacturer who supplied the item (or a typical manufacturer of who has confirmed the design requirements, in the case of two or more sources of the same line item). The manufacturer is the company or government activity exercising design control over the item; or a government specification or standard or filly coordinated industry specification or standard (e.g., FED, MIL, JAN, AN, NEMA, SAE) including type designator which completely identifies the item including its physical, mechanical, fictional, and dimensional characteristics (e.g., type, style, class, grade, series, size). Such numbers submitted via SSRs must be completely item identifying and acceptable as reference numbers in the Federal Catalog System as RNVC 2 and RNCC 2, 3, 5, or 6; RNVC 1 items may also be submitted when fill descriptive data are provided with the SSR. Non-receipt of the field descriptive data for RNVC 1 items will result in rejection of supply support.
Materiel Management Aggregation Code	A two-position alphabetic code used by the Air Force to identify specific NSNs to be managed by a specific manager.
MOE Rule Number	A four-character alphanumeric code which represents a specific MOE rule number that applies to the management of an item or a group of items of supply. The first position identifies the service/agency responsible for establishing and maintaining the MOE rules. The remaining three positions are non-significant and are used for sequencing purposes only. (See Chapter 6 of Volume 13 of Reference (f).)
NSN	The thirteen-character number which identifies the item of supply on an SSR. The first four digits, positions 8–11, are the FSC and the next nine digits, positions 12–20, are the NIIN.
Numbers of SSRs Enclosed	The quantity of different ISNs being sent to the integrated materiel manager (four characters, numeric).
Participating Service	The Service(s) which uses a multi-purpose system or equipment and obtains support for it from the Executive Service.
PC	A one-character code used to denote changes and/or relationships between NSNs and information type data. (See Table 52 of Volume 10 of Chapter 3 of Reference (f).)

Table 3. SSR Data Elements, Continued

DATA ELEMENT CODE	DATA ELEMENT DESCRIPTION
PCC	A three-character code assigned by the Service responsible for support of an end item. This code is required as a positive control feature in data processing and to ensure that data exchanges between activities may be related to the same end item. The provisioning activity or commodity manager will assign this code to a single provisioning projector program and will not use the same code to identify a different project within the contract life of the project to which it is first assigned. The code may be numeric, alphabetic, or combined alphanumeric and will be used by the SSR submitters and integrated materiel managers to continuously exchange data regarding provisioning actions, supply support status, or contract status of a given end item.
PDSSR	Designed for SSR submitters to furnish initial and EDFP or other program data, and changes thereto, concerning the end item for which supply support is being requested.
Percentage of End Items East	A two-digit figure to denote the percentage of end items which will be delivered to or deployed from East of the Mississippi River. Use 99 to indicate 100 percent. (Percentage of end item to the West Coast will be the difference between this figure and 100 percent.)
PLT	A two-digit number expressing the equal or estimated number of months' time interval between the placement of a contract and receipt into the supply system of material purchased. If less than 1 month, indicate 01 for 1 month.
Quantity Per End Item	A four-digit figure indicating the total number of times the line item is used in the end item. This legend will be completed from right to left and any spaces not used will contain a zero. If more than 9999 items are installed in the end items, indicate 9999, the maximum number permitted by the form. For incremental or component provisioning the total number of times the item is used in the increment will be indicated.
Reference Number Category Code (RNCC)	A one-digit alphanumeric code that designates the relationship of the reference number to the item of supply. (See Table 6 of Chapter 3 of Reference (f).) The appropriate RNCC for the manufacturer's P/N provided in positions 8–39 of the LISSR will be entered in positions 54 of the LISSR with DIC CXG (not used in SSR submission to Service integrated materiel manager).

Table 3. SSR Data Elements, Continued

DATA ELEMENT CODE	DATA ELEMENT DESCRIPTION
Retail Quantity	A five-digit numeric figure indicating the quantity of items required from the integrated materiel manager distribution system at the specified DRPR in the PDSSR to satisfy initial service support requirements. This includes quantities to outfit or increase levels in all organizational, intermediate, and depot-level activities supporting the end item and all other quantities intended to be requisitioned by the using Military Service in support of the end item.
RNJC	A code used to record the degree of research conducted and the justification for adding a reference number, reinstatement of an item identification, or assignment of a new NIIN despite a recognized condition of possible duplication with an existing item. (See Table 4 of Chapter 3 of Volume 10 of Reference (f).)
RNVC	A numeric code which indicates that a cited reference number is item identifying, is not item identifying, or is a reference number for information only. (See Table 7 of Chapter 3 of Volume 10 of Reference (f).) Not used in SSR submission to Service integrated materiel manager.
Shelf-life Code	Codes indicating the storage time period of a perishable item. (See Table 50 of Chapter 3 of Volume 10 of Reference (f).) Type I - An item of supply which is determined through an evaluation of technical test data and/or actual experience to be an item with a definite non-extendible period of shelf-life. Type II - An item of supply having an assigned shelf-life time period that may be extended after completion of inspection/test/restorative action.
Standard Inter-service Agency Serial Control Number (SIASCN)	The SIASCN is an alpha prefix followed by six numerics that may be assigned to Condition-3 types SSRS by the SSR submitter. The integrated materiel manager will use the SIASCN as the document control serial number (DCSN) of the FLIS transaction requesting NSN assignment and user registration.

Table 3. SSR Data Elements, Continued

DATA ELEMENT CODE	DATA ELEMENT DESCRIPTION
TDJC	A one-character alphabetic code utilized to indicate a specific reason for not furnishing technical data with Condition-3 SSRs submitted. (Not used in SSR submissions to Service integrated materiel manager.) The Services and Defense Agencies will furnish technical data with each item coded to an integrated materiel manager. However, there are circumstances when these data cannot be furnished. The following coded reasons, when applicable, will be indicated on LISSRS furnished to integrated materiel managers (DLA and/or GSA):

CODE	EXPLANATION
A	The contractor refused to accept a contract for the end item equipment with provisions for furnishing to the Government for retention, technical data (with or without limited rights provisions), and the contract was negotiated without these provisions.
B	The contract for the end item equipment was issued with provisions omitted for furnishing technical data and the contractor has refused to negotiate an amendment or a separate contract for providing these technical data.
C	Same as B except that the contractor has agreed to furnished technical data for provisioning (with or without limited rights provisions) but the price quoted for these data has been determined to be excessive when compared to potential savings that would accrue to the Government.
D	The contract contains provisions for finishing technical data (with or without limited rights provisions), and the contractor has defaulted.
E	Same as D except that the contractor has been unable to comply with terms of the contract because of subcontractor/vendor/supplier refusal to finish these data.
F	Technical data were finished with a previously submitted SSR package. Identification of the previously submitted SSR package will be provided on a separate sheet of paper.
X	Other – A detailed justification statement for non-submission of technical data will be provided on a separate sheet of paper submitted for each SSR coded X and will be appropriately cross-referenced, i.e., PC, DOR, ACF, ISN.

Table 3. SSR Data Elements, Continued

DATA ELEMENT CODE	DATA ELEMENT DESCRIPTION
TOCC	A one-character alphabetic code that identifies a new submission or a change applicable to an original submission. The codes are:

CODE	EXPLANATION
C	Changes in quantities to increase retail or wholesale quantity.
D	Deleted part but not superseded by another part. Fill retail and wholesale quantity field legends with zeros.
H	Reduction of previously submitted SSR requirements. The revised quantities are entered in the retail and wholesale quantity fields as applicable.
N	Original submission of complete provisioning or other program data and SSRs for a PCC or an increment within a PCC under which more than one increment may be submitted reflecting a different DOR (PDSSR only).
P	Design or program change to an original submission under the same PCC (PDSSR only).
R	Superseded part. The revised quantity to support the original requirement is reduced and will be entered in the retail and wholesale quantity field legends, as applicable. If the original requirement is completely deleted, the retail and wholesale quantity field legends will be filled with zeros. Must be accompanied by a TOCC S transaction.
S	Superseding part. Provides total required quantities of superseding item.
T	Technical or clerical errors other than retail and wholesale quantity field legends. Applicable only to technical or clerical errors detected on previous submissions for which acceptance response has been received from an integrated materiel manager. For retail and wholesale quantity field legends, TOCC C or D will be used to either increase or decrease quantity field legends. TOCC T will not be used for resubmission of a reject.
V	A non-provisioning SSR that provides requirements for items not originally provisioned that are generated from requisition processing or requests for support from field activities.

DATA ELEMENT CODE	DATA ELEMENT DESCRIPTION
Transaction Number	Numerals 1 and 2 are used in the LISSR only to identify transaction 1 and transaction 2 used in a CXB SSR.

Table 3. SSR Data Elements, Continued

DATA ELEMENT CODE	DATA ELEMENT DESCRIPTION

UI	A code indicating the physical measurement, the count, or, when neither is applicable, the container or shape of an item for purposes of requisitioning by and issue to the end user and is that element of management data to which the price is described. (See Table 53 of Chapter 3 of Volume 10 of Reference (f).)
	    a. The established integrated materiel manager UI will be used for items already managed by the integrated materiel manager (Condition 1) and the retail and wholesale quantities must be in terms of one-for-one relating to the UI.
	    b. For items new to IMM, the SSR submitters use the UI in LISSRs which represents the item to be supplied whether definitive or non-definitive. Particularly, if the item is to be issued by container, configuration, or other non-definitive UI, the non-definitive UI should be used and the retail and wholesale quantities and U/P should be directly related on a one-for-one basis.

U/P	A seven-digit numeric figure to indicate the actual or estimated U/P of the UI. The first two columns from the right will be cents and mills will be rounded off to the nearest cent. The next five columns will be dollars and any spaces not used will contain a zero. The minimum unit price will be 0000001 indicating 1 cent.
Wholesale Quantity	A five-digit numeric figure. The total quantity (exclusive of the retail quantity) of the item which the SSR submitter anticipates will be required for replenishment from the integrated materiel manager distribution system during the first year of operation of the end items provisioned or other projects. The quantity will assist the integrated materiel manager in requirements computations to ensure that adequate wholesale back-up stocks are available until normal demand patterns are established.
WSDC	A two-position alphanumeric code utilized to identify a specific item (spare or repair part) to the weapon system or end item of equipment to which it has application for the requirement being submitted on the SSR. A WSDC will be assigned to each weapon system entered in the Weapon System Support Program.

Table 4. PDSSR

SSR SUBMITTER TO IMM CARD COLUMNS	DATA ELEMENT	*/M/ O/C	DATA ENTRY INSTRUCTIONS
1-3	DIC	*	Enter Code W/CWA.

Table 4. PDSSR, Continued

SSR SUBMITTER TO IMM CARD COLUMNS	DATA ELEMENT	*/M/ O/C	DATA ENTRY INSTRUCTIONS
4-5	ACT	*	Enter code of recipient.
6	Rerouting Indicator	C	Enter R if the SSRs in this package have been rerouted (passed) to the correct integrated materiel manager. Otherwise leave blank.
7	TOCC	M	Enter letter N,P, or V.
8-20	End Item NSN or End Item Name, Type, or Model Number (one required)	M	Enter NSN from left to right (when available). If no NSN is available, enter end item name and type or model number. Leave unused portion blank.
21-24	Date NSNs required	O	Enter date if NSNs are required in less than 75 days after receipt of the request by the integrated materiel manager. Otherwise leave blank.
25-28	DRPR	M	Enter date.
29-48	Contract/Control Number	O	Enter the document contract/control number, when applicable, left to right. Leave unused portion blank.
49-52	DOR	*	For TOCC N and V submissions, enter the date the PDSSR is sent. For TOCC P submissions, enter the date the original PDSSR was sent.
53-56	End Item Delivery Code	O	Enter code prescribed in definitions, Table 3 of this Volume.
(53)	(Calendar Year)	O	(Enter last digit of calendar year.)
(54)	(Calendar Year Quarter)	O	(Enter numeral 1, 2, 3, or 4.)
(55-56)	(Number of Months in Delivery Cycle)	O	(Enter number of months. Enter zeros if end items have been delivered.)
57-59	PCC	*	Enter assigned code.
60-64	CAGE Code	M	Enter the code of the manufacturer of the end item.
65-68	WSDC	O	Enter appropriate code.
67-68	ACF	*	Enter the code of the originator.
69			Leave blank.

Table 4. PDSSR, Continued

SSR SUBMITTER TO IMM CARD COLUMNS	DATA ELEMENT	*/M/ O/C	DATA ENTRY INSTRUCTIONS
70-74	End Item Quantity	M	Enter the quantity of end items to be supported from right to left. Unused portion fill with zeros. (May be zero-filled for NSA end items.)
75-78	Number of SSRS Enclosed	O	Enter quantity from right to left. Unused portion fill with zeros.
79-80	Percent of End Items East	M	Enter the percentage fight to left. Unused portion fill with zeros. (May be zero-filled for NSA end items.)
* - Indicates a mandatory control element, specified data must be entered and will be used to uniquely identify an SSR. M – Indicates a mandatory data element, specified data must be entered. O – Indicates an optional data element, specified data may be entered at discretion of originator. C – Indicates a conditional data element.			

Table 5. LISSR – Condition 1

SSR SUBMITTER to IMM CARD COLUMNS	DATA ELEMENT	*/M/ O/C	DATA ENTRY INSTRUCTIONS
1-3	DIC	*	Enter Code W/CXA
4-5	ACT	*	Enter code of recipient
6			Leave blank
7	TOCC	C	Enter TOCC V when cc 7 of the PDSSR is V. When cc 7 of the PDSSR is P, enter the appropriate code from Table 3.
8-20	NSN	M	For TOCC N, S, or V submissions, enter NSN in cc 8-20. For TOCCs, C, D, H, R, and T, reproduce from original SSR.

Table 5. LISSR – Condition 1, Continued

SSR SUBMITTER to IMM CARD COLUMNS	DATA ELEMENT	*/M/ O/C	DATA ENTRY INSTRUCTIONS
21-24	MOE Rule	C	Enter MOE Rule of SSR submitter. (Only required for Service integrated materiel manager) transaction when SSR is not recorded in the DID TIR.) Leave blank for integrated materiel manager (DLA/GSA).
25-29	Retail Quantity	M	For TOCC, N, S, or V submissions, enter quantity from right to left. Fill unused portion with zeros.
30	IMC	C	Enter IMC if not previously IM coded by submitting Service (SSR submitter to integrated materiel manager (DLA and/or GSA) only).
31	Recommend AAC	O	The requestor may recommend a method of management. Otherwise leave blank. If retail/replenishment quantities reflect all zeros, enter a J.
32-36	Wholesale Quantity	M	For TOCC N, S, or V submissions, enter quantity from right to left. Fill unused portion with zeros.
37-40	Quantity Per End Item	C	For TOCC, N, S, or V submissions, enter quantity from right to left. Fill unused portion with zeros. For TOCC C, D, H, R, and T, leave blank.
41-42			Leave blank.
43-48	ISN	*	For N or V submissions, enter characters from left to right. Leave unused portion blank. For TOCC C, D, H, R, S, or T, reproduce from original SSR.
49-52	DOR	*	For N or V submissions, enter SSR is sent. (For TOCCS C, D, H, R, S, and T, reproduce from original SSR.)
53-54	UI	M	For Nor V submissions and TOCC S, enter appropriate abbreviation. For TOCC C, D, H, R, or T, reproduce from original SSR.
55	Essentiality Code	O	Enter appropriate code from Table 3 of this Volume.
56			Leave blank.
57-59	PCC	*	Enter assigned code.

Table 5. LISSR – Condition 1, Continued

SSR SUBMITTER to IMM CARD COLUMNS	DATA ELEMENT	*/M/ O/C	DATA ENTRY INSTRUCTIONS
60-61	II Data Receiver Code	O	Enter Activity Code (Army and Navy only – submit to Service integrated materiel manager only). Not required for activities already recorded in the FLIS.
62-63	11 Data Collaborator Code	O	Enter Activity code (Navy only – submit to Service integrated materiel manager only. Not required for activities already recorded in the FLIS TIR).
64			Leave blank.
65-66	Interchangeability	O	Enter appropriate code from definitions in Table 3 for TOCC R and S cards only. Otherwise leave blank.
67-68	ACF	*	Enter the code of the originator.
69-70	Materiel Management Aggregation Code (Air Force Use)	O	Air Force SSR submittals to Air Force integrated materiel manager.
	Additional II Data Code (Navy use)	O	Navy SSR submittals to Navy integrated materiel manager.
	Maintenance Code	O	SSR submittals to integrated materiel manager (DLA/GSA) must either enter the maintenance code or leave blank.
70-71	11 Data Receiver	O	Navy SSR to integrated materiel manager (Navy may add an additional receiver if required. All others leave blank).
72-73	11 Data Collaborator Code	O	Navy SSR to Service integrated materiel manager may add an additional collaborator if required. All others leave blank.
74-80			Leave blank.

* - Indicates a mandatory control element, specified data must be entered and will be used to uniquely identify an SSR.
M – Indicates a mandatory data element, specified data must be entered.
O – Indicates an optional data element, specified data may be entered at discretion of originator.
C – Indicates a conditional data element.

Table 6. LISSR – Condition 2

SSR SUBMITTER TO IMM CARD COLUMNS	DATA ELEMENT	*/M/ O/C	DATA ENTRY INSTRUCTIONS
1-3	DIC	*	Enter code W/CXA for NSN.
4-5	ACT	*	Enter code of the recipient.
6			Leave blank.
7	TOCC	C	Enter TOCC V when cc 7 of the PDSSR is V. When 7 of the PDSSR is P, enter appropriate code from definitions in Table 3 of this Volume.
8-20	NSN	M	For TOCC N, S, or V submissions, enter NSN in cc 8-20; for TCC C, D, H, R, and T, reproduce from original SSR.
21-24	MOE Rule	C	SSR submitter to Service integrated materiel manager only. Enter MOE rule of SSR submitter (not required for integrated materiel manager (DLA/GSA) transactions).
25-29	Retail Quantity	M	For TOCC N, S, or V submissions, enter quantity from right to left. Fill unused portion with zeros.
30	IMC	C	Enter IMC if not previously IM coded by submitting Service (SSR submitter to integrated materiel manager (DLA and/or GSA) only).
31	Recommended AAC	O	The requestor may recommend a method of management. Otherwise leave blank. If retail/replenishment quantities reflect all zeros, enter a J.
32-36	Wholesale Quantity	M	For TOCC, N, S, or V submissions, enter quantity from right to left. Fill unused portion with zeros.
37-40	Quantity Per End Item	C	For TOCC N, S, or V submissions, enter quantity from right to left. Filled unused portion with zeros. For TOCCs C, D, H, R, and T, leave blank
41-42	Source Code	M	For TOCC N, S, or V submissions, enter appropriate code from Table 3 of this Volume.
43-48	ISN	*	Enter character from left to right. Leave unused portion blank. For TOCC C, D, H, R, S, or T reproduced from original SSR.

Table 6. LISSR – Condition 2, Continued

SSR SUBMITTER TO IMM CARD COLUMNS	DATA ELEMENT	*/M/ O/C	DATA ENTRY INSTRUCTIONS
49-52	DOR	*	For N or V submissions, enter date SSR is sent. For TOCC C, D, H, R, S, or T, reproduce from original SSR.
53-54	UI	M	For TOCC N, S, or V submissions, enter appropriate abbreviation.
55	EC	O	Enter appropriate code from Table 3 of this Volume.
56	Demilitarization Code	M	Enter appropriate code from Table 3 of this Volume.
57-59	PCC	*	Enter assigned code.
60-61	II Data Receive Code	O	Enter activity code for Army and Navy SSR submitters to integrated materiel manager (Service) only. Not required for other SSRs or transactions to integrated materiel manager (DLA and/or GSA).
62-63	II Data Collaborator Code	O	Enter activity code (Navy SSR submitters to Service integrated materiel manager only). Not required for other SSRs or transactions to integrated materiel managers (DLA and/or GSA).
64	AMC	M	Enter code from Table 3 of this Volume.
65-66	Interchangeability Code	O	Enter appropriate code from Table 3 of this Volume or TOCC R and S cards only. Otherwise leave blank.
67-68	ACF	*	Enter the code of the originator.
69-70	Maintenance Code	O	Enter code from Table 3 of this Volume.
71	Shelf-Life Code	M	For TOCC N, S, or V submissions, enter appropriate code from Table 3 of this Volume.
72-73	PLT	M	For TOCC N, S, or V submissions, enter number of months from right to left. Fill unused portion with zeros.
74-80	U/P	M	For TOCC N, S, or V submissions, enter price in dollars and cents from right to left. Fill unused portion with zeros.

* - Indicates a mandatory control element, specified data must be entered and will be used to uniquely identify an SSR.
M – Indicates a mandatory data element, specified data must be entered.
O – Indicates an optional data element, specified data may be entered at discretion of originator.
C – Indicates a conditional data element.

Table 7. LISSR – Condition 3 (Card 1)

SSR SUBMITTER TO IMM CARD COLUMNS	DATA ELEMENT	*/M/ O/C	DATA ENTRY INSTRUCTIONS
1-3	DIC	*	Enter code W/CXB.
4-5	ACT	*	Enter code of recipient.
6	Card Number	M	Enter numeral 1.
7	TOCC	O	Enter TOCC V when cc 7 of the PDSSR is V. When cc 7 of the PDSSR is P, enter appropriate code from Table 3 of this Volume.
8-13			Leave blank.
14-20	SIASCN	C	Mandatory for Joint Service provisioning; may also be used in single Service provisioning/non-provisioning.
21-24	MOE Rule	C	SSR submitter to Service integrated materiel manager only. Enter MOE rule of SSR submitter.
25-29	Retail Quantity	M	For TOCC N, S, or V submissions, enter quantity from right to left. Fill unused portion with zeros.
30	IMC	C	SSR submitter to integrated materiel manager (DLA/GSA) only. For TOCC N, S, or V submissions, enter applicable code. For TOCC C, D, H, R, or T, reproduce from original SSR. (Not used in LISSRs from SSR submitter to Service integrated materiel manager.)
31	Recommended AAC	O	The requestor may recommend a method of management. Otherwise leave blank. If retail/replenishment quantities reflect all zeros, enter a J.
32-36	Wholesale Quantity	M	For TOCC N, S, or V submissions, enter quantity from right to left. Fill unused portion with zeros.
37-40	Quantity, Per End Item	C	For TOCC, C, S, or V submissions, enter quantity from right to left. Fill unused portion with zeros.
41-42	Source Code	M	Enter appropriate code from Table 3 of this Volume.

Table 7. LISSR – Condition 3 (Card 1), Continued

SSR SUBMITTER TO IMM CARD COLUMNS	DATA ELEMENT	*/M/ O/C	DATA ENTRY INSTRUCTIONS
43-48	ISN	*	Enter characters from left to right. Leave unused portion blank. For TOCC C, D, H, R, S, or T, reproduce from original SSR.
49-52	DOR	*	For N or V submissions, enter date SSR is sent. For TOCC C, D, R, S, or T, reproduce from original SSR.
53-54	UI	M	For TOCC, N, S, or V submissions, enter appropriate abbreviation.
55	EC	O	Enter appropriate code from Table 3 of this Volume.
56	Demilitarization Code	M	Enter appropriate code from Table 3 of this Volume.
57-59	PCC	*	Enter assigned code.
60-61	11 Data Receiver Code	O	Enter code for Army and Navy SSR submitters to Service integrated materiel manager only.
62-63	11 Data Collaborator Code	O	Enter code for Navy SSR submitters to Service integrated materiel manager only. Not required for other SSRs or transactions to integrated materiel managers (DLA and/or GSA).
64	AMC	M	Enter code from Table 3 of this Volume.
65-66	Interchangeability Code	O	Enter appropriate code from the definitions in Table 3 of this Volume for TOCC R and S cards only. Otherwise leave blank.
67-68	ACF	*	Enter code of SSR submitter.
69-70	Maintenance Code	O	Enter code from Table 3 of this Volume.
71	Shelf-Life Code	M	For TOCC N, S, or V submissions, enter appropriate code.
72-73	PLT	M	For TOCC N, S, or V submissions, enter number of months from right to left. Fill unused portion with zeros.
74-80	U/P	M	For TOCC N and S submissions, enter price in dollars and cents from right to left. Fill unused portion with zeros.

* - Indicates a mandatory control element, specified data must be entered and will be used to uniquely identify an SSR.

M – Indicates a mandatory data element, specified data must be entered.

O – Indicates an optional data element, specified data may be entered at discretion of originator.

C – Indicates a conditional data element.

Table 8. LISSR – Condition 3 (Card 2)

SSR SUBMITTER TO IMM CARD COLUMNS	DATA ELEMENT	*/M/ O/C	DATA ENTRY INSTRUCTIONS
1-3	DIC	*	Enter code W/CXB.
4-5	ACT	*	Enter Activity code of the recipient of the SSR.
6	Card Number	M	Enter numeral 2.
7	TOCC	C	Enter code from cc 7 of card 1.
8-39	Manufacturer's P/N	M	For TOCC N, S, or V submissions, enter characters from left to right. Leave unused portion blank.
40-42			Leave blank.
43-48	ISN	*	Reproduce from Card Number 1. Enter characters from left to right. Leave unused portion blank.
49-52	DOR	*	For Nor V submissions, reproduce from card number 1. For TOCC C, D, H, R, S, or T, reproduce from original SSR.
53	AMSC	M	Enter appropriate code from Table 3 of this Volume.
54	RNCC	C	Enter appropriate code from Table 3 of this Volume. (Not required for Service integrated materiel manager or when technical data is provided integrated materiel manager (DLA and/or GSA).)
55	RNVC	C	Enter appropriate code from Table 3 of this Volume. (Not required for Service integrated materiel manager or when technical data is provided integrated materiel manager (DLA and/or GSA).)
56	DAC	C	Enter appropriate code from Table 3 of this Volume. (Not required for Service integrated materiel manager or when technical data is provided integrated materiel manager (DLA and/or GSA).)
57-59	PCC	*	Enter assigned code
60-64	CAGE Code	M	Enter manufacturer's code relating to part number in cc 8-39
65-66			Leave blank.
67-68	ACF	*	Enter code of originator.

Table 8. LISSR – Condition 3 (Card 2), Continued

SSR SUBMITTER TO IMM CARD COLUMNS	DATA ELEMENT	*/M/O/C	DATA ENTRY INSTRUCTIONS
69-72	DTDS	C	Enter data technical data will be supplied, if known. (Completed only when data is not sent with SSR.). If date is known, leave blank and complete cc 73. (SSR submitter to integrated materiel manager (DLA and/or GSA) only).
73	TDJC	C	Leave blank cc 69-72 are filled. Not required for integrated materiel manager transactions or if technical data is sent with the SSR.
74	RNJC	C	For TOCC N, S, or V submissions, enter the appropriate numeric code only when the item of supply/production submitted is identified as a possible or probable match of NSN in FLIS TIR which is not technically acceptable.
75-80			Leave blank.

* - Indicates a mandatory control element, specified data must be entered and will be used to uniquely identify an SSR.
M – Indicates a mandatory data element, specified data must be entered.
O – Indicates an optional data element, specified data may be entered at discretion of originator.
C – Indicates a conditional data element.

Table 9. Additional Reference Number – DIC CXG

SSR SUBMITTER TO CIMM CARD COLUMNS	DATA ELEMENT	*/M/O/C	DATA ENTRY INSTRUCTIONS
1-3	DIC	*	Enter code CXG.
4-5	ACT	*	Enter code of the recipient.
6-7			Leave blank.
8-39	Reference Number	M	Enter number from left to right. Leave unused portion blank. Numbers exceeding 32 positions are not acceptable.
40-42			Leave blank.
43-48	ISN	*	Enter same number as shown on applicable CXA, CXB, or CXC card(s).
49-52	DOR	*	Enter same number as shown on applicable CXA, CXB, or CXC card(s).

Table 9. Additional Reference Number – DIC CXG, Continued

SSR SUBMITTER TO CIMM CARD COLUMNS	DATA ELEMENT	*/M/ O/C	DATA ENTRY INSTRUCTIONS
53			Leave blank.
54	RNCC	C	Enter code. Not required if technical data for the reference number are sent with this card.
55	RNVC	C	Enter code. Not required if technical data for the reference number are sent with this card.
56	DAC	C	Enter code. Not required if technical data for the reference number are sent with this card.
57-59	PCC	*	Enter same code shown in applicable CXA, CXB, or CXC card(s).
60-64	CAGE Code	M	Enter manufacturer's code relating to part number in cc 8-39.
65-66			Leave blank.
67-68	ACF	*	Enter code of the originator.
69-80			Leave blank.

* - Indicates a mandatory control element, specified data must be entered and will be used to uniquely identify an SSR.
M – Indicates a mandatory data element, specified data must be entered.
O – Indicates an optional data element, specified data may be entered at discretion of originator.
C – Indicates a conditional data element.

Table 10. Additional User – DIC CXK

SSR SUBMITTER TO CIMM CARD COLUMNS	DATA ELEMENT	*/M/ O/C	DATA ENTRY INSTRUCTIONS
1-3	DIC	*	Enter code CXK.
4-5	ACT	*	Enter code of the recipient.
6-7			Leave blank.
8-9	Additional User	M	Enter in cc 8-9 the activity code of the additional user. SSR submitter to integrated materiel manager (DLA and/or GSA) only.
10-29			Leave blank.
30	IMC		Enter IMC if not previously IMC. Otherwise leave blank.
31-42			Leave blank.

Table 10. Additional User – DIC CXK, Continued

SSR SUBMITTER TO CIMM CARD COLUMNS	DATA ELEMENT	*/M/ O/C	DATA ENTRY INSTRUCTIONS
43-48	ISN	*	Enter same number as shown on CXA, CXB, or CXC card(s).
49-52	DOR	*	Enter same date as shown on applicable CXA, CXB, or CXB card(s).
53-56			Leave blank.
57-59	PCC	*	Enter code shown on CXB card(s).
60-66			Leave blank.
67-68	ACF	*	Enter code of the originator.
69-80			Leave blank.

* - Indicates a mandatory control element, specified data must be entered and will be used to uniquely identify an SSR.
M – Indicates a mandatory data element, specified data must be entered.
O – Indicates an optional data element, specified data may be entered at discretion of originator.
C – Indicates a conditional data element.

Table 11. Item Name Card – DIC CXF

SSR SUBMITTER TO CIMM CARD COLUMNS	DATA ELEMENT	*/M/ O/C	DATA ENTRY INSTRUCTIONS
1-3	DIC	*	Enter code CXF.
4-5	ACT	*	Enter code of the recipient.
6			Leave blank.
7	TOCC	C	Enter S if TOCC S item meets need for submission of item name card, otherwise leave blank.
8-42	Item Name	M	Enter item name and modifiers from left to right. Leave unused portion blank. Continue overflow into cc 69-80.
43-48	ISN	*	Enter code shown on CXB cards.
49-52	DOR	*	Enter same date shown on applicable CXB cards.
53-56	FSC	M	Enter code for the item.
57-59	PCC	*	Enter same code shown on applicable CXB cards.
60-66			Leave blank.

Table 11. Item Name Card – DIC CXF, Continued

SSR SUBMITTER TO CIMM CARD COLUMNS	DATA ELEMENT	*/M/ O/C	DATA ENTRY INSTRUCTIONS
67-68	ACF	*	Enter code of the originator.
69-80	Item Name Overflow	C	Enter overflow of item name.
* - Indicates a mandatory control element, specified data must be entered and will be used to uniquely identify an SSR. M – Indicates a mandatory data element, specified data must be entered. O – Indicates an optional data element, specified data may be entered at discretion of originator. C – Indicates a conditional data element.			

Table 12. LIAC Final Positive Advice

SSR SUBMITTER TO CIMM CARD COLUMNS	DATA ELEMENT	*/M/ O/C	DATA ENTRY INSTRUCTIONS
1-3	DIC	*	Enter code CXI.
4-5	ACT	*	Enter code of the recipient.
6			Leave blank.
7	TOCC	C	If original SSR contained a V, then reproduce it here; otherwise leave blank.
8-20	NSN	M	Enter NSN.
21-29			Leave blank.
30	AAC	M	Enter code under which item will be supported.
31-42			Leave blank.
43-48	ISN	*	Reproduce from original SSR.
49-52	DOR	*	Reproduce from original SSR.
53-56	DADV	M	Enter date of transmittal.
57-59	PCC	*	Reproduce from original SSR.
60-64			Leave blank.
65-66	ATC	M	Enter YA, YB, YD, YE, or YX as applicable.
67-68	ACF	*	Enter code of originator.
69-76			Leave blank.

Table 12. LIAC Final Positive Advice, Continued

SSR SUBMITTER TO CIMM CARD COLUMNS	DATA ELEMENT	*/M/ O/C	DATA ENTRY INSTRUCTIONS
77-80	Support Date	C	Enter appropriate date if ATC in cc 65-66 of this transaction is YX.
* - Indicates a mandatory control element, specified data must be entered and will be used to uniquely identify an SSR. M – Indicates a mandatory data element, specified data must be entered. O – Indicates an optional data element, specified data may be entered at discretion of originator. C – Indicates a conditional data element.			

Table 13. LIAC Integrated Materiel Manager-to-SSR Submitter Interim Advice

SSR SUBMITTER TO CIMM CARD COLUMNS	DATA ELEMENT	*/M/ O/C	DATA ENTRY INSTRUCTIONS
1-3	DIC	*	Enter code CX1.
4-5	ACT	*	Enter code of recipient.
6			Leave blank.
7	TOCC	C	If original SSR contained V, then reproduce it here; otherwise leave blank.
8-42	(8-20) NSN -or-	C	Use NSN if ATC is YG, YH,YJ, YL, or YR.
	(8-39) P/N –or-		Enter P/N if ATC is YF or YQ.
	(8-42) Blank		Leave blank if ATC is YC, YK, YT, YU, YY, YZ.
43-48	ISN	*	Reproduce from original SSR.
49-52	DOR	*	Reproduce from original SSR.
53-56	DADV	M	Enter date of transmittal.
57-59	PCC	*	Reproduce from DIC CX3.
60-64	CAGE Code	C	Enter CAGE code if ATC is YF or YQ; otherwise leave blank.
65-66	ATC	M	Enter YC, YF, YG, YH, YJ, YK, YL, YQ, YR, YT, YU, YW, YY, or YZ as applicable.
67-68	ACF	*	Enter code off originator.
69	AAC	C	Enter code of replacement item if ATC is YJ or YR.
70	ISC	C	Enter code of replacement if ATC is YJ or YR.

Table 13. LIAC Integrated Materiel Manager-to-SSR Submitter Interim Advice, Continued

SSR SUBMITTER TO CIMM CARD COLUMNS	DATA ELEMENT	*/M/O/C	DATA ENTRY INSTRUCTIONS
71	PC	C	Enter PC of replacement item if ATC is YJ, YR, YW.
72-74			Leave blank.
75-76	Activity Code Passed To	C	Enter the code of the integrated materiel manager to which the SSR has been passed if the ATC is YC, YK, or YU; otherwise leave blank.
77-80	FSC	C	All numeric if ATC is TC; otherwise leave blank.

* - Indicates a mandatory control element, specified data must be entered and will be used to uniquely identify an SSR.
M – Indicates a mandatory data element, specified data must be entered.
O – Indicates an optional data element, specified data may be entered at discretion of originator.
C – Indicates a conditional data element.

Table 14. LIAC Integrated Materiel Manager-to-SSR Submitter Reject Advice

SSR SUBMITTER TO CIMM CARD COLUMNS	DATA ELEMENT	*/M/O/C	DATA ENTRY INSTRUCTIONS
1-3	DIC	*	Enter code CX1.
4-5	ACT	*	Enter code of recipient.
6			Leave blank.
7	TOCC	C	If original SSR contained a V, then reproduce it here; otherwise leave blank.
8-42			Leave blank.
43-48	ISN	*	Reproduce from original SSR.
49-52	DOR	*	Reproduce from original SSR.
53-56	DADV	M	Enter date of transmittal.
57-59	PCC	*	Reproduce from original SSR.
60-64			Leave blank.
65-66	ATC	M	Enter applicable numeric ATC. If ATC is 36, a DIC CX5 may accompany this transaction.
67-68	ACF	*	

Table 14. LIAC Integrated Materiel Manager-to-SSR Submitter Reject Advice, Continued

SSR SUBMITTER TO CIMM CARD COLUMNS	DATA ELEMENT	*/M/ O/C	DATA ENTRY INSTRUCTIONS
69-80			Leave blank.
* - Indicates a mandatory control element, specified data must be entered and will be used to uniquely identify an SSR. M – Indicates a mandatory data element, specified data must be entered. O – Indicates an optional data element, specified data may be entered at discretion of originator. C – Indicates a conditional data element.			

Table 15. LIAC SSR Submitter-to-Integrated Materiel Manager Reply to Offer

SSR SUBMITTER TO CIMM CARD COLUMNS	DATA ELEMENT	*/M/ O/C	DATA ENTRY INSTRUCTIONS
1-3	DIC	*	Enter code CX2.
4-5	ACT	*	Enter code of recipient.
6-42			Leave blank.
43-48	ISN	*	Reproduce from original SSR.
49-52	DOR	*	Reproduce from original SSR.
53-56	DADV	M	Enter date of transmittal.
57-59	PCC	*	Reproduce from original SSR.
60-64			Leave blank.
65-66	ATC	*	Enter YM or YN.
67-68	ACF	M	Enter code or originator.
69-80		*	Leave blank.
* - Indicates a mandatory control element, specified data must be entered and will be used to uniquely identify an SSR. M – Indicates a mandatory data element, specified data must be entered. O – Indicates an optional data element, specified data may be entered at discretion of originator. C – Indicates a conditional data element.			

Table 16. LIAC SSR Submitter-to-Integrated Materiel Manager Follow-Up

SSR SUBMITTER TO CIMM CARD COLUMNS	DATA ELEMENT	*/M/ O/C	DATA ENTRY INSTRUCTIONS
1-3	DIC	*	Enter code CX3.

Table 16. LIAC SSR Submitter-to-Integrated Materiel Manager Follow-Up, Continued

SSR SUBMITTER TO CIMM CARD COLUMNS	DATA ELEMENT	*/M/O/C	DATA ENTRY INSTRUCTIONS
4-5	ACT	*	Enter code of recipient.
6-42			Leave blank.
43-48	ISN	*	Reproduce from original SSR.
49-52	DOR	*	Reproduce from original SSR.
53-56	DADV	M	Enter date of transmittal.
57-59	PCC	*	Reproduce from original SSR.
60-66			Leave blank.
67-68	ACF	*	Enter code of originator.
69-80			Leave blank.

* - Indicates a mandatory control element, specified data must be entered and will be used to uniquely identify an SSR.
M – Indicates a mandatory data element, specified data must be entered.
O – Indicates an optional data element, specified data may be entered at discretion of originator.
C – Indicates a conditional data element.

Table 17. LIAC Reply to DIC CX3 Follow-Up

SSR SUBMITTER TO CIMM CARD COLUMNS	DATA ELEMENT	*/M/O/C	DATA ENTRY INSTRUCTIONS
1-3	DIC	*	Enter code CX4.
4-5	ACT	*	Enter code of recipient.
6-7			Leave blank.
8-20	NSN		Enter NSN which will support this SSR requirement.
21-29			Leave blank.
30	AAC	C	Enter code under which SSR is supported if ATC shows positive final advice.
31-42			Leave blank.
43-48	ISN	*	Reproduce from DIC CX3.
49-52	DOR	*	Reproduce from DIC CX3.
53-56	DADV	M	Enter date of transmittal
57-59	PCC	*	Reproduce from DIC CX3
60-64			Leave blank.

Table 17. LIAC Reply to DIC CX3 Follow-Up, continued

SSR SUBMITTER TO CIMM CARD COLUMNS	DATA ELEMENT	*/M/ O/C	DATA ENTRY INSTRUCTIONS
65-66	ATC	M	Enter code assigned this SSR from provisioning records; enter ATC 66 only if no record found.
67-68	ACF	*	Enter code of originator.
69-80			Leave blank.
* - Indicates a mandatory control element, specified data must be entered and will be used to uniquely identify an SSR. M – Indicates a mandatory data element, specified data must be entered. O – Indicates an optional data element, specified data may be entered at discretion of originator. C – Indicates a conditional data element.			

Table 18. LIAC Additional Data Card for ATC 36 Rejects

SISR SUBMITTER TO CIMM CARD COLUMNS	DATA ELEMENT	*/M/ O/C	DATA ENTRY INSTRUCTIONS
1-3	DIC	*	Enter code CX5.
4-5	ACT	*	Enter code of recipient.
6-42	Reason of Return	M	In-the-clear text message indicating reason for rejection.
43-48	ISN	*	Reproduce from original SSR.
49-52	DOR	*	Reproduce from original SSR.
53-56	DADV	M	Enter date of transmission.
57-59	PCC	*	Reproduce from original SSR.
60-65			Leave blank.
66	Overflow Indicator	O	Enter alpha Y to indicate additional information to explain rejection will be forwarded by mail on DD Form 2241.
67-68	ACF	*	Enter code of originator.
69-80	Continuation Field	O	Fill if cc 6-42 does not provide enough room for message.
* - Indicates a mandatory control element, specified data must be entered and will be used to uniquely identify an SSR. M – Indicates a mandatory data element, specified data must be entered. O – Indicates an optional data element, specified data may be entered at discretion of originator. C – Indicates a conditional data element.			

Table 19. LIAC Quality Requirement Card

SSR SUBMITTER TO IMM CARD COLUMNS	DATA ELEMENT	*/M/ O/C	DATA ENTRY INSTRUCTIONS
1-3	DIC	*	Enter code CXT.
4-5	ACT	*	Enter code of the recipient.
6-7			Leave blank.
8-20	NSN	C	Enter NSN (when available). If no NSN is available, complete cc 21-33.
21-26	ISN	*	Enter characters from left to right. Leave unused portion blank.
27-30	Date of Request	*	Enter date SSR is sent.
31-33	Provisioning	*	Enter code assigned.
34-40			Leave blank.
41	Item Technical Description or Off-the-Shelf	C	Enter code to indicate whether item is commercial Military-Federal (FAR/DoD FAR Supplement 46.203 (Reference (h)).) Enter a "C" if commercial (catalogs, drawings, industrial standards), an "M" for Military-Federal (drawings, specifications), or "O" for off-the-shelf (contractor may produce the items to either commercial or Military-Federal item specifications or descriptions).
42	Type of Item	M	Enter code ("C" or "S") to indicate whether item is complex ("C") or noncomplex ("S"). Complex items have quality characteristics, not wholly visible in the end item for which contractual conformance must progressively be established through precise measurements, tests and controls accomplished during purchasing, in manufacturing, assembly, and fictional operations either as an individual item or in conjunction with other items. For noncomplex items, simple measurement and test of the end item is sufficient to determine conformance to contract requirements.
43	Type of Critical Application	M	Enter code ("P" or "C") to indicate whether item is peculiar (item has only one application) or common (item has multiple applications).
44			Leave blank.
45-65	Equipment/System Application	O	Enter name of major assembly or end item and weapon system code (cc 63-65).

Table 19. LIAC Quality Requirement Card, continued

SSR SUBMITTER TO IMM CARD COLUMNS	DATA ELEMENT	*/M/ O/C	DATA ENTRY INSTRUCTIONS
66			Leave blank.
67	Transfer of Technical Data Availability	M	Enter "A" if data is available. Enter "N" if data is not available.
68	Location	M	Enter "L" data is located at losing item manager or "R" if located at the Repository.
69	Limited Rights	C	Enter "G" if Government has limited rights.
70	Adequate for MFG	C	Enter "M" if data has been determined to be adequate for manufacturing the item.
71-74	Transferred to DLA	M	Enter date (month, last 2 digits of year) technical data was transferred to DLA. If not transferred, enter an "N" in cc 71.
75-76	ACF	*	Enter code of the originator.
77-80			Leave blank.

* - Indicates a mandatory control element, specified data must be entered and will be used to uniquely identify an SSR.

M – Indicates a mandatory data element, specified data must be entered.

O – Indicates an optional data element, specified data may be entered at discretion of originator.

C – Indicates a conditional data element.

Table 20. LIAC Out-year Requirement Card

SSR SUBMITTER TO IMM CARD COLUMNS	DATA ELEMENT	*/M/ O/C	DATA ENTRY INSTRUCTIONS
1-3	DIC	*	Enter code CFR.
4-5	ACT	*	Enter code of recipient.
6-9	DRPR	M	Enter DRPR. Must agree with the DRPR on the PDSSR.
10			Leave blank.
11-16	Second Year Retail Quantity	M	Enter the retail quantity required for support 13-24 months after the DRPR. Fill unused portion with zeros.
17-22	Second Year Replenishment	M	Enter the replenishment quantity required for support 13-24 months after the DRPR. Fill unused portion with zeros.

Table 20. LIAC Out-year Requirement Card, Continued

SSR SUBMITTER TO IMM CARD COLUMNS	DATA ELEMENT	*/M/ O/C	DATA ENTRY INSTRUCTIONS
23			Leave blank.
24-29	Third Year Retail Quantity	M	Enter the retail quantity required for support 25-36 months after the DRPR. Fill unused portion with zeros.
30-35	Third Year Replenishment Quantity	M	Enter the replenishment quantity required for support 25-36 months after the DRPR. Fill unused portion with zeros.
36			Leave blank.
37-42	Fourth Year Quantity	M	Enter the retail quantity required for support 36-48 months after the DRPR. Fill unused portion with zeros.
43-48	Fourth Year Replenishment Quantity	M	Enter the replenishment quantity required for support 37-48 months after the DRPR. Fill unused portion with zeros.
49			Leave blank
50-55	Fifth Year Retail Quantity	M	Enter the retail quantity required for support 49-60 months after the DRPR. Fill unused portion with zeros.
56-61	Fifth Year Replenishment Quantity	M	Enter the replenishment quantity required for the support 49-60 months after the DRPR. Fill unused portion with zeros.
62			Leave blank.
63-66	DOR	*	Enter number shown on CXA, B, or C, transaction.
67-68	ACF	*	Enter code of originator.
69-74	ISN	*	Enter number shown on CXA, B, or C, transaction.
75-77	PCC	*	Enter number shown on CXA, B, or C, transaction.
75-80			Leave blank.

* - Indicates a mandatory control element, specified data must be entered and will be used to uniquely identify an SSR.
M – Indicates a mandatory data element, specified data must be entered.
O – Indicates an optional data element, specified data may be entered at discretion of originator.
C – Indicates a conditional data element.

Table 21. Data Distribution List for Notification of Repetitive Demands for Non-registered Users

SERVICE/ AGENCY	TYPE OF DATA TO BE DISTRIBUTED	DISTRIBUTION LIST
Army	Transactions by electronic transmission	Commander USAMC Logistics Support Activity ATTN: AMXLS-MD Redstone Arsenal, AL 35898-7466 Communications Routing Identifier: RUDQCDA
Army	A listing of Army Security Assistance Program (SAP) requisitions, which the Army is not to be recorded as a user in the FLIS database	Commander U.S. Army Security Affairs Command ATTN: AMSAC New Cumberland, PA 17070-5096
Navy	Transactions by electronic transmission, excluding non-NSN P/N medical items and FSC 9150 and 9160 items	U.S. Army Security Assistance Command ATTN: AMSAC New Cumberland, PA 17070-5096
Navy	Listings for non-NSN P/N medical items	Commanding Officer Navy Medical Logistics Command Attn: Code 4 Fort Detrick, MD 21702
Navy	Listings for FSC 9150 and 9160	Naval Operational Logistics Support Center (NOLSC) Petroleum 8725 John J. Kingman Rd. Suite 3719 Fort Belvoir, VA 22060-6224
Navy	Listings non-NSN P/N JZ items	Commanding Officer Navy Inventory Control Center Attn: Code 85413 5450 Carlisle Pike P.O. Box 2020 Mechanicsburg, PA 17055
Marine Corps	Listings	Commanding General Marine Corps Logistics Bases Integrated Logistics Support Directorate (Code 850) 814 Radford Blvd Albany, GA 31704-1128 Communications Routing Identifier: RUQABNB

Table 21. Data Distribution List for Notification of Repetitive Demands for Non-registered Users, Continued

SERVICE/ AGENCY	TYPE OF DATA TO BE DISTRIBUTED	DISTRIBUTION LIST
Air Force	Transactions by electronic transmission (except for 2 and 3 below)	AF Global Logistics Support Center 401 SCMS/GUMB 4375 Chidlaw Road Wright-Patterson AFB, OH 45433 Communications Routing Identifier: RUWTUAC
Air Force	Listing of FSG 68 and FSG 91 items on which the Air Force is not recorded as a user	AFPET/AFTH 2430 C. Street, Area B, Bldg 70, Rm 114 Wright-Patterson AFB, OH 45433-7632
Air Force	A listing of Air Force SAP requisitions on which the Air Force is not recorded as a user	AF Global Logistics Support Center 401 SCMS/GUMB 4375 Chidlaw Road Wright-Patterson AFB, OH 45433
USCG	Listings	Commandant U.S. Coast Guard Headquarters ATTN: G-ELM-2 2100 2d Street, SW Washington, DC 20593-0001 Communications Routing Identifier: RUCGWAA
FAA	Listings	Federal Aviation Administration Mike Monroney Aeronautical Center ATTN: AAC-490 P.O. Box 25082 Oklahoma City, OK 73125 Communication Routing Identifier: RUWTEHA
NSA	Listings	Director National Security Agency ATTN: L161 Fort George G. Meade, MD 20755-6000 Communication Routing Identifier: RUETIAA

Table 21. Data Distribution List for Notification of Repetitive Demands for Non-registered Users, Continued

SERVICE/ AGENCY	TYPE OF DATA TO BE DISTRIBUTED	DISTRIBUTION LIST
NWS	Listings	NEXRAD Joint System/Program Office National Weather Service ATTN: NWS-OSO322 Room 326 8060 13th Street Silver Spring, MD 20910 Communication Routing Identifier: RUEAHQA

Table 22. NSN Format for Automatic Recording of User Interest Notification

Field Legend	Position	Explanation
DIC	1-3	This field will contain the appropriate code to identify the type of transaction.
		Enter DIC WZ 1 to indicate that adoption action has been initiated.
		Enter DIC WZ2 to indicate information for referral and review by appropriate SICA.
IMM Activity Code	4-5	Originating Activity Code.
Service/Agency Activity Code	6-7	Receiving Service/AAC Activity Code.
Requisitioned NSN	8-22	Enter from the requisition.
Blank	23-27	Leave blank.
Unit of Issue	28-29	Enter the requisition. (Positions 23-24)
Quantity	30-34	Enter from the requisition. (Positions 25-29)
Document Number	35-48	Enter from the requisition. (Positions 30-43)
Demand Code	49	Enter from the requisition. (Position 44)
Supplementary Address	50-55	Enter from the requisition. (Positions 45-50)
Distribution Code	56-58	Enter from the requisition. (Positions 54-56)
Project Code	59-61	Enter from the requisition. (Positions 57-59)
Priority Designator Code	62-63	Enter from the requisition.
ATC	64-65	Enter "IS" to that action has been initiated to register the appropriate activities in both the nonstandard NSN in positions 8-22 and the standard NSN in positions 67-79. Enter "S1" to that action has been initiated to register the appropriate activities in DLIS only on the standard NSN in positions 67-79.
Blank	66	Leave blank.

Table 22. NSN Format for Automatic Recording of User Interest Notification, Continued

Field Legend	Position	Explanation
Standard NSN	67-79	Enter the standard NSN, when applicable.
Continuation Indicator Code	80	Enter a dash (-) if additional records for NSN (position 8-22) follow. If record for the item, leave blank.
Header/Trailer - AUTODIN header and trailer records will be applied in accordance with JANAP 128. A unique content indicator code "IHFM" will be assigned to positions 5-8. The communication routing identifier (positions 10- 16) will identify the originating integrated materiel manager. The communication routing identifier (positions 41-47) will identify the intended recipient.		

Table 23. Non-NSN Part Number Format for Automatic Recording of User Interest Notification

Field Legend	Position	Explanation
DIC	1-3	This field will contain the appropriate code to identify the type of transaction.
		Enter DIC WZ 3 for notification that P/N qualified for NSN.
		Enter WZ4 for notification that stock number request (LN___) transaction has been forwarded to DLIS.
		Enter DIC WZ5 for notification of the NSN assigned to the P/N in positions 8-22 and 23-27.
		Enter DIC WZ6 to indicate information for referral and review by appropriate SICA. See Advice code in positions 64-65.
		Enter DIC WZ7 for notification that an existing NSN has been identified/adopted for the P/N item requisitioned.
IMM Activity Code	4-5	Originating activity code
Service/Agency Activity Code	6-7	Receiving Service/AAC Activity code
Requisitioned Manufacturer's Code and Part Number	8-22	Mandatory. Enter from the requisition (DD Form 1348-6).
Manufacturer's Code and P/N Overflow Field	23-27	Enter from the requisition (DD Form 1348-6).
Unit of Issue	28-29	Enter the requisition. (Positions 23-24)
Quantity	30-34	Enter from the requisition. (Positions 25-29)
Document Number	35-48	Enter from the requisition. (Positions 30-43)
Demand Code	49	Enter from the requisition. (Position 44)

Table 23. Non-NSN Part Number Format for Automatic Recording of User Interest Notification, Continued

Field Legend	Position	Explanation
Supplementary Address	50-55	Enter from the requisition. (Positions 45-50)
Distribution Code	56-58	Enter from the requisition. (Positions 54-56)
Project Code	59-61	Enter from the requisition. (Positions 57-59)
Priority Designator Code	62-63	Enter from the requisition (Positions 60-61)
Advice Code	64-65	For WZ6, enter one of the following Advice codes: X1 – FSC not applicable to processing integrated materiel manager. X2 – Non-consumable item X3 – Restricted FSC
Reference Identification Code	66	For WZ3/WZ6, enter one of the following codes (if applicable) from the requisition (position 70) to identify the entry in positions 67-79. A – Technical Order or Manual B – End Item Identification C – Noun Description of Item D – Drawing or Specification Number
Reference Identification or NSN (Applicable DICs) or	67-79	Enter the information from positions 71-80 of the Identification or requisition or the NSN assigned to the item.
Document Control Serial Number (DCSN) and Federal Supply Class (FSC) (Applicable DIC WZ4)* or	67-79	See below
DCSN	67-73	Enter DCSN from NSN request transaction for the involved P/N.
Blank	74	Leave blank.
FSC	75-78	Enter FSC assigned to P/N.
Blank	79	Leave blank.
Continuation Indicator Code	80	Enter a dash (-) if additional records for NSN (position 8-22) follow. If last record for the item, leave blank.
Header/Trailer – Apply AUTODIN header and trailer records in accordance with JANAP 128. Assign a unique content indicator code "IHFM" to positions 5-8. The Communication Routing Identifier (positions 10-16) identifies the originating integrated materiel manager. The Communication Routing Identifier (positions 41-47) identifies the intended recipient. (* Use when providing notification with DIC WZ4)		

Table 24. NSN Listing Format for Automatic Recording of User Interest Notification

Field Legend	Position	Explanation
DIC	1-3	This field will contain the appropriate code to identify the type of transaction.
		Enter DIC WZ1 to indicate that adoption action has been initiated.
		Enter DIC WZ2 to indicate information for referral and review by appropriate SICA.
Blank	4-5	Leave blank.
IMM Activity Code	6-7	Originating integrated materiel manager Activity code – Mandatory.
Blank	8-10	Leave blank.
Service/AAC	11-12	Receiving Service/Agency activity code – Mandatory.
Blank	13-15	Leave blank.
Requisitioned NSN	16-30	Mandatory.
Blank	31-33	Leave blank.
Unit of Issue	34-35	Mandatory.
Blank	36-38	Leave blank.
Quantity	39-43	Mandatory.
Blank	44-46	Leave blank.
Document Number	47-60	Mandatory.
Blank	61-63	Leave blank.
Demand Code	64	Mandatory.
Blank	65-67	Leave blank.
Supplementary Address	68-73	If available.
Blank	74-76	Leave blank.
Distribution Code	77-79	If available.
Blank	80-82	Leave blank.
Project Code	83-85	If available.
Blank	65-67	Leave blank.
Priority Designator code	89-90	Mandatory.*
Blank	91-100	Leave blank.
Advice Code	101-102	Mandatory.
Blank	103-110	Leave blank
Standard NSN	111-123	If appropriate.
Blank	124-130	Leave blank.

For those activities not utilizing electronic transmission processing, the integrated materiel manager will provide listings containing the data in the same record formats.

* Not required for semiannual listings for medical, clothing and textile, and Military-distinctive items.

Table 25. Non-NSN Part Number Listing Format for Automatic Recording of User Interest Notification

Field Legend	Position	Explanation
DIC	1-3	This field will contain the appropriate code to identify the type of transaction.
		Enter DIC WZ3 for notification that P/N qualifies for NSN.
		Enter DIC WZ4 for notification that stock number request (LN) transaction has been forwarded to DLIS.
		Enter DIC WZ5 for notification of the NSN assigned to the P/N in positions 16-30 and 34-38.
		Enter DIC WZ6 to indicate information for referral and review by appropriate SICA. See advice code in positions 97-98.
		Enter DIC WZ7 for notification that an existing NSN has been identified/adopted for the P/N item requisitioned-Mandatory.*
Blank	4-5	Leave blank.
IMM Activity Code	6-7	Originating integrated materiel manager activity code – Mandatory.
Blank	8-10	Leave blank.
Service/AAC	11-12	Receiving Service/Agency Activity code - Mandatory.
Blank	13-15	Leave blank.
Requisitioned Manufacturer's Code and P/N	16-30	Mandatory.
Blank	31-33	Leave blank.
Manufacturer's Code and Part Number Overflow Field	34-38	If available.
Blank	39	Leave blank.
Unit of Issue	40-41	Mandatory.
Blank	42	Leave blank.
Quantity	43-47	Mandatory.
Blank	48-49	Leave blank.
Document Number	50-63	Mandatory.
Blank	64-66	Leave blank.
Demand Code	67	Mandatory.
Blank	68-70	Leave blank.
Supplementary Address	71-76	If available.
Blank	77-79	Leave blank.
Distribution code	80-82	If available.

Table 25. Non-NSN Part Number Listing Format for Automatic Recording of User Interest Notification, Continued

Field Legend	Position	Explanation
Blank	83-85	Leave blank.
Project Code	86-88	If available.
Blank	89-91	Leave blank.
Priority Designator Code	92-93	Mandatory.
Blank	94-96	Leave blank.
Advice Code	97-98	For WZ6, enter applicable advice code X1, X2, X3 (See definitions in App-M-2)
Blank	99-101	Leave blank.
Reference Identification Code	102	For WZ3/WZ6, enter reference identification ode from requisition, if applicable.
Blank	103-105	Leave blank.
Reference/NSN/DCSN/FSC	106-118	For WZ3/WZ6, enter reference identification from the requisition. For WZ4, enter the DSN in positions 106-112 and the FSC in positions 114-117 from the cataloging request for NSN assignment. For WZ5/WZ7, enter the NSN assigned for (or matched to) the requisitioned part number.
Blank	119-130	Leave blank.
For those activities not utilizing electronic transmission processing, the integrated materiel manager will provide listings containing the data in the same record formats.		
*Not required for semiannual listings for medical, clothing and textile, and Military-distinctive items.		

Table 26. Automatic Recording of User Interest DICs

DIC	DESCRIPTION
WZ1	Identifies the transmission that an adoption action has been initiated by the integrated materiel manager.
WZ2	Identifies that the transmission contains information for referral and review by the SICA.
WZ3	Identifies the transmission of a notification to the SICA that a P/N qualifies for NSN assignment.
WZ4	Identifies the transmission of a notification to the SICA that a stock number request (LN___) transaction has been forwarded to DLIS.
WZ5	Identifies the transmission of a notification to the SICA of the NSN assigned to the part number in positions 8-22 and 23-27.
WZ6	Identifies the transmission contains information for referral and review by the SICA.

Table 26. Automatic Recording of User Interest DICs, Continued

DIC	DESCRIPTION
WZ7	Identifies the transmission of a notification that an existing NSN has been identified and/or adopted for the part number requisitioned.
The DICs prescribed herein are 3-character alphanumeric codes which identify automatic recording of user interest notifications.	

ENCLOSURE 4

SSR CONTROL ELEMENTS AND TIMEFRAME OBJECTIVES

1. <u>SSR CONTROL ELEMENTS</u>. SSR submitters and/or integrated materiel managers will use the controlling elements in this section for both processing and controlling SSR transactions. These control elements will be used to detect or prevent duplicate SSR submissions. (A PCC/ISN/DOR combination will not be duplicated by a single SSR submitting activity while the PCC resides in any SSR files at that activity.) The control elements to be included in all SSR transactions are:

    a. DIC

    b. ACT

    c. ISN

    d. DOR

    e. PCC

    f. ACF

2. <u>ALLOWED TIMES</u>

    a. Objectives for completion of key events are contained in Table 27.

    b. SSR submitter and/or integrated materiel manager processing systems will provide for both external and internal functional follow-ups when processing actions are overdue. External functional follow-ups will be generated and transmitted under the allowed timeframes. Internal functional follow-up/notification will require action to correct the error condition, provide the required advice, or take other appropriate action to complete processing for any exceptional conditions.

Table 27. SSR Timeframe Objectives

SSR EVENT	START	STOP	OBJECTIVE (DAYS)
Deliver SSR to integrated materiel manager	DOR [1]	Receipt by integrated materiel manager	15
Deliver EDFP to integrated materiel manager	DOR	Receipt by integrated materiel manager	15
Final Advice, P/N SSR	Receipt by integrated materiel manager of SSR	Receipt by SSR submitter	60 [2,3,4]
Final Advice, NSN SSR	Receipt by integrated materiel manager of SSR	Receipt by SSR submitter	25
Offer	Receipt by integrated materiel manager of SSR	Receipt by SSR submitter	30
Deliver EDFP for Offered Item to SSR Submitter	Transmission Date of DIC CX1, ATC YQ	Receipt by SSR submitter	15
SSR Submitter Reply of Offer	Receipt by SSR submitter of offer (YL/YQ)	CX2 received by integrated materiel manager	75
Follow-up Generated by SSR submitter – P/N SSR	DOR	Follow-up generated	65
Follow-up Generated by SSR Submitter – NSN SSR	DOR	Follow-up generated	30
Offer Follow-up by integrated materiel manager	Date of advice	Follow-up generated	55

[1] DOR will not be earlier than 15 days before receipt of the SSR by integrated materiel manager.
[2] Add 30 days to the objective if the SSR is rerouted (interim YC, YK).
[3] Add 75 days to the objective if alternate/substitute item is offered (interim ATC YL, YQ).
[4] Add 105 days to the objective if a request for NSN must be submitted to a NATO country other than the United States (interim ATC YH).

ENCLOSURE 5

USE OF SIASCN

1. <u>USE OF SIASCN IN SSRs</u>. A SIASCN must be used in SSRs being submitted during joint Service provisioning. It is also appropriate for use during single Service provisioning. The SIASCN will be identified for all P/N SSRs being submitted by the Service assigned executive management responsible for multi-Service provisioning. SIASCN identification for P/N SSRs submitted for single Service provisioning will be a Service option. The integrated materiel manager will use the SIASCN as the DCSN of the FLIS transaction requesting NSN assignment and user registration.

2. <u>EXECUTIVE SERVICE</u>

a. The Service designated as the Executive Service will assign the SIASCN to items requiring NSN assignment during joint Service provisioning coordination with the participating Military Departments. The Military Department conducting single Service provisioning will assure the assignment of the SIASCN, as required.

b. The SIASCN will be composed of a specific alphabetic prefix designating the Executive Service and followed by six numbers. The six-position numeric will be developed to preclude assignment of the same SIASCN to two or more items. The alphabetic prefixes in Table 28 will be assigned to the SIASCN by the Executive Service in coordination with the participating Military Department or by the designated Service provisioning activities.

Table 28.   Alphabetic Prefixes Assigned to SIASCN

SERVICE	INVENTORY CONTROL POINT (ICP) MANAGING ACTIVITY	PREFIX
Marine Corps	PA	A
Air Force	TD	Q
	TG	C
	SU	E
	SX	F
	SJ	J
Army	AJ	B
	AZ	K
	BD	L
	BF	M
	CT	N

<u>Table 28</u>. <u>Alphabetic Prefixes Assigned to SIASCN</u>, Continued

SERVICE	INVENTORY CONTROL POINT (ICP) MANAGING ACTIVITY	PREFIX
	CU	P
	CM	U
Navy	HD	H, T
	HX	X
	JV	S
	KE	R
Prefix Z reserved for expansion.		

    c. The SIASCN will be recorded on P/N SSRs submitted by the Executive Service when submitting an SSR. Add user (DIC CXK) may be submitted for either joint Service or single Service provisioning.

    d. The SIASCN will be placed in the P/N SSRS (DIC CXB) transaction 1, positions 14-20.

    e. SSRs being submitted by the designated Executive Service will provide consolidated wholesale or retail requirements for all users.

    f. Submit SSRS for design change notices (DCNs) or program changes under the procedures identified in section 4 of Enclosure 3 of this Volume. The participating Military Departments will be notified in advance of the SSRs of any changes to the equipment by copies of the DCNs or a follow-on provisioning conference, if required.

3. <u>PARTICIPATING SERVICE</u>

    a. The SIASCN assigned by the Executive Service during the provisioning meeting or conference will be recorded by the participating Service on internal control files for use in updating records upon assignment of the NSN.

    b. Submit SSRs identifying any requirements not included in the SSR submitted by the Executive Service.

    c. Submit SSRs for items unique to a participating Service.

    d. All SSRs will be submitted under the established procedures (e.g., TOCC N).

    e. The participating Service will submit SSRs for all items identifying both wholesale and retail quantities when buying equipment previously provisioned by an Executive Service.

4. <u>INTEGRATED MATERIEL MANAGERS' USE OF SIASCN</u>. Integrated materiel managers will

    a. Upon receipt of a P/N SSR containing a SIASCN, ensure the SIASCN is used as the DCSN of the FLIS transaction requesting NSN assignment and user registration. This process will permit participating Military Departments to identify notification of NSN assignment and the appropriate management data from the DLIS notification for all P/N SSRs submitted during the joint Service provisioning.

    b. Furnish LIAC to the Executive and/or submitting Service.

    c. Add the appropriate MOE Rule or supplementary data receiver code for all participating Military Departments identified by the Executive Service on DIC CXK.

    d. Periodically provide to the Executive and participating Military Departments, at their request, status reports on all SSRs submitted for joint Service provisioning.

GLOSSARY

PART I. ABBREVIATIONS AND ACRONYMS

AAC	Acquisition Advice Code
ACT	activity code to
ACF	activity code from
AMC	Acquisition Method Code
AMSC	Acquisition Method Suffix Code
ASD(L&MR)	Assistant Secretary of Defense for Logistics and Materiel Readiness
ATC	action taken code
CAGE	commercial and Government entity
DADV	date of advice
DCN	Design Change Notice
DCSN	Document Control Serial Number
DIC	Document Identifier Code
DISA	Defense Information Systems Agency
DLA	Defense Logistics Agency
DLIS	DLA Logistics Information Service
DoDD	Department of Defense Directive
DOR	date of request
DRPR	date repair parts required
DTDS	date technical data to be supplied
DTRA	Defense Threat Reduction Agency
EC	essentiality code
FAA	Federal Aviation Administration
FAR	Federal Acquisition Regulation
FLIS	Federal Logistics Information System
FMS	Foreign Military Sales
FSC	Federal Supply Classification
GIM	Gaining Inventory Manager
GSA	General Services Administration
ICP	Inventory Control Point
IEC	Item Entry Code
IMC	item management code
IMM	integrated materiel management
ISC	item standardization code
ISN	item serial number

LIAC	line item advice code
LIAT	line item advice transaction
LIM	Losing Inventory Manager
LISSR	line item supply support request
LR	logistics reassignment
MOE	major organization entity
NATO	North Atlantic Treaty Organization
NCB	National Codification Bureau
NI	not interchangeable
NIIN	national item identification number
NSA	National Security Agency
NSN	National Stock Number
NWS	National Weather Service
PC	phrase code
PCC	provisioning control code
PDSSR	program data supply support request
PLT	production lead time
P/N	part number
RNCC	reference number category code
RNJC	reference number justification code
RNVC	reference number variation code
SAP	security assistance program
SIASCN	standard inter-service agency control number
SICA	secondary inventory control point
EDFP	supplemental data for provisioning
SPTD	supplementary provisioning technical documentation
SSR	supply support request
TDJC	technical data justification code
TIR	total item record
TOCC	type of change code
UI	unit of issue
U/P	unit price
USCG	United States Coast Guard
USD(AT&L)	Under Secretary of Defense for Acquisition, Technology, and Logistics
WSDC	weapon system designator code

PART II. DEFINITIONS

These terms and their definitions set forth standard terminology for use in DoD supply chain materiel management.

AAC. A code denoting how, as distinguished from where and under what restrictions, an item will be acquired.

ATC. A 2-character alphabetic or numeric code to identify advice being provided in a LIAT.

CAGE code. A 5-digit code that combines the FSC for manufacturers and the FSC for non-manufacturers of the end items or parts.

consumable item. An item of supply or an individual item (except explosive ordnance and major end items of equipment) that is normally expended or used up beyond recovery in the use for which it is designed or intended.

duplicate SSR. A duplicate SSR is a submitted SSR reflecting the same control elements, including DOR, as on a previously submitted SSR.

engineering data for provisioning. Technical data which provides definitive identification of dimensional, material, mechanical, electrical, and/or other characteristics that depict the physical characteristics, location, and function of the item.

Executive Service. The Service that is formally designated, assigned responsibility, and delegated authority for life cycle management for a multi-Service system or equipment jointly used by two or more Military Departments.

green product. A product that exhibits the environmentally positive characteristics of an environmental organization approved through the DLA-chaired Joint Group on Environmental Attributes, and has a lesser or reduced effect on human health and the environment when compared to competing products or services that serve the same purpose.

ICP. An organizational unit or activity within the DoD supply system that is assigned the primary responsibility for the materiel management of a group of items either for a particular Military Service or Department or for the Department of Defense as a whole. In addition to IMM functions, an ICP may perform other logistics functions in support of a particular Military Service or Department or for a particular end item (e.g., centralized computation of retail requirements levels and engineering tasks associated with weapon system components).

IMC. The process of determining whether items of supply in FSC assigned for IMM qualify for management by the individual Components other than DLA or GSA.

IMM. Any activity or agency that has been assigned wholesale IMM responsibility for the Department of Defense and participating Federal Agencies. IMM responsibilities include cataloging, requirements determination, procurement, distribution overhaul, repair, and disposal of materiel.

interchangeable and substitutable family. Two or more items having interchangeable and/or substitutable relationship with another. The head of the family is called the master item, i.e., an item with an interchangeable or substitutable relationship with every member of the family.

inventory. Materiel, titled to the U.S. Government, held for sale or issue, held for repair, or held pending transfer to disposal

item of supply. A category of items identified by an NSN with the same form, fit, and function. The individual items (units) included in this category could be manufactured by multiple sources.

LR. The transfer of IMM responsibilities from one manager to another.

materiel. Defined in Joint Publication 1-02 (Reference (j)).

materiel management. Continuing actions relating to planning, organizing, directing, coordinating, controlling, and evaluating the application of resources to ensure the effective and economical support of military forces. It includes provisioning, cataloging, requirements determination, acquisition, distribution, maintenance, and disposal. The terms "materiel management," "materiel control," "inventory control," "inventory management," and "supply management" are synonymous.

MOE. The principal subdivision of Government organization under which component organization entities are identified (e.g., Army, Navy, Air Force, Marine Corps, DLA, NSA, GSA).

MOE Rule. Codes reflecting the relationship of an activity to an item of supply. The codes are defined in Volume 13 of Reference (f).

non-consumable items of supply. NSN items of supply that are major end items, depot-reparable components, or special management items.

repetitive demand items. Items for which two or more requisitions are recorded within a 180-day period on NSNs or P/N items where the participant is not a recorded user.

retail. Level of inventory below the wholesale level, either at the consumer level for the purpose of directly providing materiel to ultimate users, or at the intermediate or region level for the purpose of supplying consumer levels or ultimate users in a geographical area.

retail quantity. Retail quantity is a five-digit numeric figure indicating the quantity of items required from the IMM Distribution System during the first year of operation of the end item provisioned commencing with the date repair part required. This includes quantities to outfit or increase levels in all organizational, intermediate, and depot level activities support of weapon systems and other end items.

SSR. A transaction identifying requirements for consumable items that is submitted by the component introducing a materiel/weapon system to the integrated materiel manager.

supply chain. Defined in Reference (j).

supply chain management. Defined in Reference (j).

wholesale. The highest level of organized DoD supply, and as such, procures, repairs, and maintains stocks to resupply the retail levels of supply. The terms "wholesale supply," "wholesale level of supply," "wholesale echelon," and "national inventory" are synonymous.

wholesale or replenishment quantity. Wholesale or replenishment quantity is a five-digit numeric figure that the customer anticipates will be required for replenishment from the IMM distribution system during the first year of operation. This quantity is exclusive of the retail quantity of the item that the customer anticipates will be required for replenishment from the IMM distribution system during the first year of operation of the end items provisioned or other projects. This quantity assists the integrated materiel manager in requirements computations to ensure that adequate wholesale backup stock is available.